OAE 019 Elementary Education Subtest II

Mathematics, Science, Arts, Health, and Fitness

By: Preparing Teachers In America™

This page is intentionally left blank.

This page is intentionally left blank.

Free Online Email Tutoring Services

All preparation guides purchased directly from Preparing Teachers In America includes a free three month email tutoring subscription. Any resale of preparation guides does not qualify for a free email tutoring subscription.

What is Email Tutoring?

Email Tutoring allows buyers to send questions to tutors via email. Buyers can send any questions regarding the exam processes, strategies, content questions, or practice questions.

Preparing Teachers In America reserves the right not to answer questions with or without reason(s).

How to use Email Tutoring?

Buyers need to send an email to onlinepreparationservices@gmail.com requesting email tutoring services. Buyers may be required to confirm the email address used to purchase the preparation guide or additional information prior to using email tutoring. Once email tutoring subscription is confirmed, buyers will be provided an email address to send questions to. The three month period will start the day the subscription is confirmed.

Any misuse of email tutoring services will result in termination of service. Preparing Teachers In America reserves the right to terminate email tutoring subscription at anytime with or without notice.

Comments and Suggestions

All comments and suggestions for improvements for the study guide and email tutoring services need to be sent to onlinepreparationservices@gmail.com.

This page is intentionally left blank.

Table of Content

This page is intentionally left blank.

About the Exam and Study Guide

What is the Elementary Education Subtest II Exam?

The Elementary Education Subtest II Exam is an exam to test potential teachers' competencies in basic knowledge necessary to pursue a teaching career in elementary education. The exam is aligned with the Common Core State Standards, and the exam covers the following content areas:

- Mathematics
- Science
- Arts, Health, and Fitness

The exam is timed at 105 minutes and consists of 75 questions. The 75 selected-response questions are based on knowledge obtained in a bachelor's degree program. The exam contains some questions that may not count toward the score.

What topics are covered on the exam?

The following are some topics covered on the exam:

- Diversity of life and adaption
- Physical and chemical properties
- Forces and motion
- Interaction of energy and matter
- Physical education and health education
- Structure of the earth
- Processes of the earth
- Functions
- Congruence, similarity, right Triangles, and circles
- Geometric measurement and dimension
- Modeling in geometry
- Basic statistics and probability

What is included in this study guide book?

This guide includes two full length practice exams for the Elementary Education Subtest II Exam along with detail explanations. The recommendation is to take the exams under exam conditions and a quiet environment.

This page is intentionally left blank.

Practice Test 1

This page is intentionally left blank.

Exam Answer Sheet Test 1

Below is an optional answer sheet to use to document answers.

Question Number	Selected Answer	Question Number	Selected Answer	Question Number	Selected Answer	Question Number	Selected Answer
1		21		41		61	
2		22		42		62	
3		23		43		63	
4		24		44		64	
5		25		45		65	
6		26		46		66	
7		27		47		67	
8		28		48		68	
9		29		49		69	
10		30		50		70	
11		31		51		71	
12		32		52		72	
13		33		53		73	
14		34		54		74	
15		35		55		75	
16		36		56			
17		37		57			
18		38		58			
19		39		59			
20		40		60			

This page is intentionally left blank.

Practice Exam 1 - Questions

QUESTION 1

Mark has a writing assignment due in 5 days. In order to complete it, he plans to write 15 pages during one day and writes 5 pages each remaining day as he proofreads. How many pages does Mark plan to write?

    A. 20
    B. 30
    C. 35
    D. 40

Answer:

QUESTION 2

The elevation h in feet as a function of time of a group of hikers as they hike in a mountain is described by h=736t+3210. The variable t is time in hours, and the function is valid when 0<t<3. Which of the following statements is the best interpretation of the number 736 in the context of this problem?

    A. The elevation of the group during the first three hours of their hike.

    B. The elevation of the group as a function of time during the first three hours of their hike.

    C. The decrease in the elevation per hour of the group during the first three hours of hiking.

    D. The increase in the elevation per hour of the group during the first three hours of hiking.

Answer:

QUESTION 3

$$-3x + 15 < 6$$

Which of the following values of x are solutions of the inequality above?

    A. 0.75

    B. 2.89

    C. 2.21

    D. 3.14

Answer:

QUESTION 4

If $\frac{3}{x-4} = \frac{5}{y}$ where y≠0 and x≠4, what is y in terms of x?

    A. $y=2x-10$

    B. $y=\frac{5}{2}x+6$

    C. $y=\frac{5}{3}x-\frac{20}{3}$

    D. $y=\frac{7}{3}x+\frac{10}{3}$

Answer:

QUESTION 5

Kyle jogs at least 20 minutes, and then, he works out for an hour and ten minutes. What is the minimum amount of time in minutes he uses to complete his physical activities?

    A. 90 minutes

    B. 100 minutes

    C. 130 minutes

    D. 150 minutes

Answer:

QUESTION 6

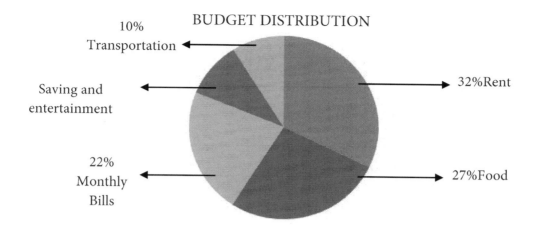

The graph above shows the percent of Mary's monthly budget distributed into her more important expenses. What percent of her monthly budget can she use for saving and entertainment?

A. 8%

B. 9%

C. 10%

D. 11%

Answer:

QUESTION 7

Tom buys a package that contains 432 marbles. If he seeks to distribute packs of 15 marbles to his classmates, what is the total number of complete packs that he can make?

A. 22

B. 28

C. 29

D. 30

Answer:

QUESTION 8

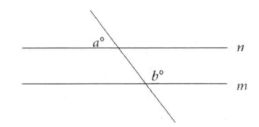

In the figure above, line n and line m are parallel, and b = 3a. What is the value of a?

A. 25°

B. 35°

C. 45°

D. 55°

Answer:

QUESTION 9

If $\frac{1}{5}x - \frac{1}{4}y = 10$, what is the value of 4x-5y?

A. 100
B. 160
C. 200
D. 240

Answer:

QUESTION 10

Month	Miles Driven
January	2600
February	3000
March	3200
April	2400
May	1800
June	
July	3400
August	3200
September	2500
October	2700
November	1900
December	2200

The table above shows the approximate number of miles driven by Bill during each month in the past year. How many miles did Bill drive during June if the arithmetic mean of the miles driven for the entire year was 2600?

A. 2300 miles

B. 2400 miles

C. 2500 miles

D. 2550 miles

Answer:

QUESTION 11

Printers A and B work together to complete an assigned job. Printer A completes this job in 8 hours. Both printers working together complete the job in 6 hours. How many hours does it take for Printer B to complete the job if it was working alone?

A. 16
B. 18
C. 20
D. 24

Answer:

QUESTION 12

In a map displaying the freeway system, 1 inch is represented by 200 miles. How many inches on the map represent a freeway of 2,460 miles of length?

A. 9.6
B. 9.8
C. 10.8
D. 12.3

Answer:

QUESTION 13

A machine can perform 40 identical tasks in 4 hours. At this rate, what is the minimum number of machines that should be assigned to complete 90 of the tasks within 2 hours?

A. 4
B. 5
C. 7
D. 8

Answer:

QUESTION 14

A certain doctor earns n dollars for each individual she consults with plus x dollars for every 15 minutes the doctor consults. If in a certain week she works 14 hours and supports 15 individuals, how much does she earn for that week, in dollars?

    A. $14n + 15$

    B. $15n \times 15x + 15$

    C. $15n + \frac{14 \times 60}{15}x$

    D. $15x + \frac{14 \times 60}{15}n$

Answer:

QUESTION 15

$$156, 176, 198, x, 165$$

The range calculated for the above data is 45. Determine the missing value, x?

    A. 111
    B. 153
    C. 178
    D. 200

Answer:

QUESTION 16

$$\sqrt{(8 \times 72)} =$$

    A. 2-
    B. 24
    C. 36
    D. 48

Answer:

QUESTION 17

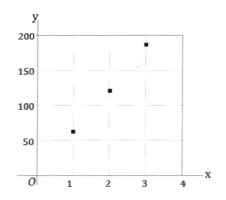

What relationship can be represented by the data points in the graph above?\

    A. hours and minutes

    B. meters and inches

    C. meters and yards

    D. weeks and months

Answer:

QUESTION 18

If x-2y=0 and -2x+y=2, then 3x-3y=

A. -4
B. -2
C. 0
D. 3

Answer:

QUESTION 19

The figure is a parallelogram. If 65 < k < 80, select all the following that could be the value of n?

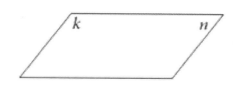

I. 89   II. 95   III. 105   IV. 107   V. 118

A. I and III
B. II and IV
C. III and IV
D. II and V

Answer:

QUESTION 20

Card Collection Data

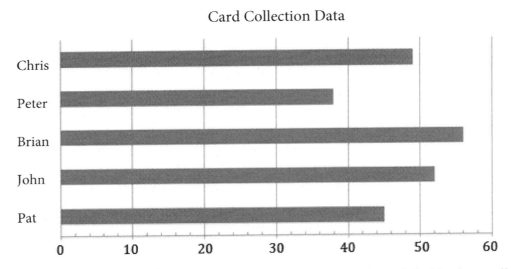

Five kids meet to play a trading card game. The number of cards each kid had initially is shown in the graph above. After the game, Pat had 28; John had 45; Brian had 52; and Chris had 63. How many cards does Peter have after the game?

    A. 10
    B. 28
    C. 38
    D. 52

Answer:

QUESTION 21

The following formula is the volume of a sphere:

$$\text{Volume of Sphere} = \frac{4}{3} \times \pi \times r^3$$

What is the volume in cubic inches of spherical balloon that has a diameter of 8 inches?

    A. $\frac{256}{3}\pi$

    B. $\frac{512}{3}\pi$

    C. $\frac{64}{3}\pi$

    D. $\frac{2048}{3}\pi$

Answer:

QUESTION 22

Brand A sells erasers in packages of 4, while Brand B sells erasers in packages of 3. If Donna buys 12 packages of Brand A, then how many packages of Brand B does she have to buy to get the same quantity?

    A. 18
    B. 16
    C. 14
    D. 12

Answer:

QUESTION 23

Which of the following numbers has a square that is less than itself?

    A. -3
    B. 0
    C. 0.3
    D. 3

Answer:

QUESTION 24

$$0.376544376544376544376544\ldots$$

In the decimal number above, the first six digits to the right of the decimal point repeat indefinitely in the same order. What is the 326th digit to the right of the decimal point?

A. 4
B. 5
C. 6
D. 7

Answer:

QUESTION 25

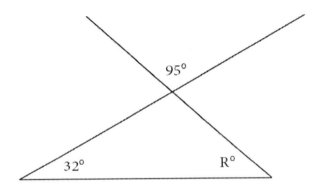

From the figure above, determine the value of the angle, R.

A. 32°
B. 37°
C. 39°
D. 53°

Answer:

QUESTION 26

In a classroom, 19 kids have at least one brother and 13 kids have at least one sister. Of the kids who have a brother or a sister, 8 have both a brother and a sister. If there are 35 kids in the class, how many kids do NOT have any siblings?

    A. 15
    B. 12
    C. 14
    D. 11

Answer:

QUESTION 27

If x is divisible by 8, then it is divisible by 6

The above statement is false, if x equals:

    A. 6
    B. 14
    C. 48
    D. 64

Answer:

QUESTION 28

Use the chart below for the next three questions.

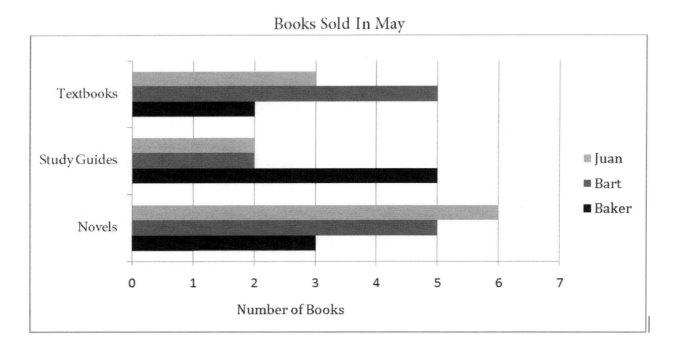

Which type of book was sold the most?

- A. Textbooks
- B. Study Guides
- C. Novels
- D. Textbooks and Novels

Answer:

QUESTION 29

The above chart shows the different types of books sold by Juan, Bart, and Baker in the month of May. What is the mean of the books sold by the three individuals?

    A. 10
    B. 11
    C. 12
    D. 13

Answer:

QUESTION 30

Of the three types of books, which of the three books contains the value of the mode?

    I.   Textbooks
    II.   Study Guides
    III. Novels

    A. II only
    B. I and II
    C. I and III
    D. I, II, and III

Answer:

QUESTION 31

Bill is ten years older than his sister. If Bill was twenty-five years of age in 1983, in what year could he have been born?

    A. 1948
    B. 1953
    C. 1958
    D. 1963

Answer:

QUESTION 32

The following are the scores Todd made on his exams during the Spring Semester: 90, 90, 90, 77, 75, 100, 84, 82 and 71. The instructor drops the two lowest scores and replaces those scores with the two highest scores. What is the average of Todd's scores?

    A. 84.33
    B. 89.22
    C. 99.22
    D. 90.00

Answer:

QUESTION 33

John had two grocery bags, and they were weighed to the nearest kilogram. The bags weighed 33kg and 43kg. If the combined weight was W kg, which is true?

    A. $76.5 \leq W \leq 77$
    B. $72 \leq W \leq 73$
    C. $74.5 \leq W \leq 75.5$
    D. $75.5 \leq W \leq 76.5$

Answer:

QUESTION 34

The width of Marty's backyard is 43.2 feet and the length is 32.1 feet. What is the area of the rectangular shaped backyard?

    A. 150.5 feet^2
    B. 160.6 feet^2
    C. 150.6 feet^2
    D. 1386.72 feet^2

Answer:

QUESTION 35

Of the following, which is/are greater than 1.25?

      I. 125%   II. 3/2   III. 150%   IV. 2/3   V. 12.5%

    A. I and II
    B. II and III
    C. II and IV
    D. III and IV

Answer:

QUESTION 36

If x is a real number and integer and completes the solution $x^4 = 16$, which statement is true?

    A. x is less than 4
    B. x is greater than 4
    C. x is less than 2
    D. x = 2

Answer:

QUESTION 37

Sports Day Teams

Number of Teams	Students Per Team
4	3
2	8
6	2

From the chart, how many total students are there?

    A. 12
    B. 13
    C. 40
    D. 44

Answer:

QUESTION 38

If the area of a triangle is $A = \frac{1}{2} \times b \times h$, then what would be the area of two triangles of the same size and shape?

A. $2 \times h$
B. $b \times h$
C. $2 \times b \times h$
D. $b^2 h^2$

Answer:

QUESTION 39

What is the main reason why no vaccine shots have been created for common cold?

A. too many causes of common cold to develop vaccine
B. common cold has to run its course
C. because it is a virus
D. it contains bacteria

Answer:

QUESTION 40

Which of the following is not considered a high cloud?

A. cirrus
B. cirrostratus
C. cirrocumulus
D. cumulus

Answer:

QUESTION 41

What is average height of an American male?

    A. 60 inches
    B. 70 inches
    C. 80 inches
    D. 90 inches

Answer:

QUESTION 42

Which of the following is the best option to weight a person?

    A. scale using lbs
    B. scale using grams
    C. dropped weight scale
    D. body mass scale

Answer:

QUESTION 43

Indigenous individuals living in the tropical regions of the world had contribution to modern science. Which practice is the most significant influence to modern science?

    A. using medicinal plants to treat illnesses
    B. developing the compass
    C. devising a plan to clean ocean water for daily use
    D. improving framing practices to better the nutrients levels of sand

Answer:

QUESTION 44

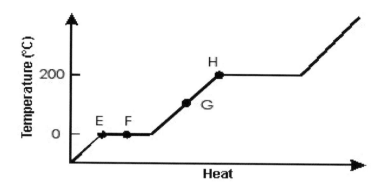

Mr. Clayton is conducting a mini experiment in which a sample of frozen water is being heated over a bunsen burner. He has documented the temperature and the heat during the experiment. The results are shown in the graph above, which shows a curve as it is heated from solid to liquid to gas phases. The beaker contains a mixture of the sample in both the solid and liquid phase at point _____.

    A. E
    B. F
    C. G
    D. H

Answer:

QUESTION 45

Marine organisms play a significant part in the existence of fossils mostly because

    A. the pressure of the ocean water destroys animal life resulting in fossils
    B. sedimentary rocks' material exist at the bottom of the ocean
    C. the high water pressure results in fossils
    D. the energy in the fossils are a result of dead marine organism

Answer:

QUESTION 46

Which of the following is the process in which rocks are broken down into smaller fragments by the atmosphere and other factors in the environment?

    A. weathering

    B. osmosis

    C. decartelization

    D. erosion

Answer:

QUESTION 47

When individuals are constantly involved in resistance weight training, they are likely to benefit the body by:

    A. decreasing chances of heart disease

    B. increasing bone density

    C. increasing blood flow

    D. decreasing joint dismemberment

Answer:

QUESTION 48

Which of the following medium results in sound to travel the fastest?

    A. air

    B. light

    C. water

    D. wire

Answer:

QUESTION 49

Which of the following is not true about arthropod?

    A. Arthropods have a segmented body, a tough exoskeleton, and jointed appendages.

    B. Arthropods are surrounded by a tough external covering, or exoskeleton.

    C. Arthropods include insects, crabs, centipedes, and spiders.

    D. Appendages are structures that do not extend from the body wall.

QUESTION 50

An early childhood teacher is having students drop common objects into a water table. The teacher has the student document which item floats or sinks. Afterwards, a discussion is held on the common properties for objects that sink and float. Which of the following concepts is best introduced with this activity?

    A. water properties

    B. density

    C. volume

    D. mass

Answer:

QUESTION 51

A cumulus cloud starts to form in a warm air mass that is ascending rapidly through a slightly cooler air mass. Of the following, which is likely the most logical cause of condensation in the warm air mass?

    A. a reduction in temperature caused by the reduction in atmospheric pressure

    B. a reduction in temperature caused by the heat transfer of two masses

    C. an increase in temperature resulting in the increase in dew point

    D. an increase in relative humidity caused on the increase in water content

Answer:

QUESTION 52

Of the following, which is considered a vertebrate?

    A. jellyfish
    B. butterfly
    C. earthworm
    D. hummingbird

Answer:.

QUESTION 53

 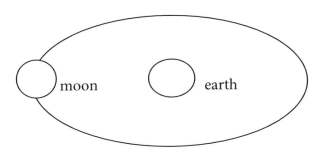

The above illustration is an example of:

    A. a solar eclipse
    B. a lunar eclipse
    C. a moon depiction
    D. earth configuration

Answer:

QUESTION 54

Data obtained for the variables x and y are collected during an experiment and given below.

X	4	8	16	20	24	28
Y	.05	.19	.33	.47	.61	.75

Which of the following best describes the relationship between x and y?

   A. linear
   B. inverse
   C. constant
   D. no relationship

Answer:

QUESTION 55

An area is most likely to experience _____ the day after a cold front passes.

   A. severe weather
   B. lower temperature
   C. cloud cover
   D. drought conditions

Answer:

QUESTION 56

Which of the following is one of the layers of Earth's atmosphere?

   A. Corona
   B. Biosphere
   C. Nebula
   D. Stratosphere

Answer:

QUESTION 57

    I.   provides the energy to move the body

    II.   provides a rigid frame that supports many organs of the body

    III.   provides oxygen storage for the body during times of strenuous exertion

Of the above, which of the following correctly states the function(s) of the human skeletal system?

    A. I only
    B. II only
    C. I and II
    D. II and III

Answer:

QUESTION 58

A storm in high plains moves toward the Mid-West. What most likely causes the storms to strengthen?

    A. air pressure
    B. clash of cold, dry air from the north
    C. wind from the west
    D. wind from the east

Answer:

QUESTION 59

    I.   A burner on a propane stove is lighted to heat water.

    II.   Boiling water is poured through a filter containing ground coffee.

Which of the following steps in making a cup of coffee involves a physical change in the matter?

    A. I only

    B. II only

    C. I and II

    D. None of the above

Answer:

QUESTION 60

    I.   A basketball thrown across a field will fall in an arc to the ground.

    II.   A hockey puck gliding on ice will continue moving until friction reduces the speed.

Which of the following statements illustrates Newton's first law of motion?

    A. I only

    B. II only

    C. I and II

    D. none of the above

Answer:

QUESTION 61

Which of the following is a renewable source of energy?

    A. biomass

    B. gas

    C. coal

    D. oil

Answer:

QUESTION 62

Water changing forms of energy due to the environment is an example of which of the following?

    A. dew on grass

    B. frost on windshield

    C. puddle in road

    D. rain cloud

Answer:

QUESTION 63

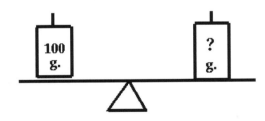

Which of the following will balance the balance scale?

    A. 10

    B. 20

    C. 50

    D. 100

Answer:

QUESTION 64

Smoking, poor nutrition, inactive, and excessive sleeping are examples of what form of health risk factors?

    A. physical fitness
    B. biological factors
    C. inherited factors
    D. behavioral factors

Answer:

QUESTION 65

    I.   transformations
    II.   translocations
    III. additions
    IV. losses

From above, which of the following is the correct order of how soil is formed?

    A. II, I, III, IV
    B. III, IV, II, I
    C. I, II, III, IV
    D. I, IV, III, II

Answer:

QUESTION 66

Which of the following correct defines how the major rocks are formed?

A.
- Sedimentary rocks – formed when magma cools and hardens
- Metamorphic rocks – formed under the surface of the earth from the metamorphosis
- Igneous rocks - formed from particles of sand, shells, and other fragments of material

B.
- Sedimentary rocks – formed under the surface of the earth from the metamorphosis
- Metamorphic rocks – formed from particles of sand, shells, and other fragments of material
- Igneous rocks - formed when magma cools and hardens

C.
- Sedimentary rocks – formed from particles of sand, shells, and other fragments of material
- Metamorphic rocks – formed when magma cools and hardens
- Igneous rocks - formed under the surface of the earth from the metamorphosis

D.
- Sedimentary rocks – formed from particles of sand, shells, and other fragments of material
- Metamorphic rocks – formed under the surface of the earth from the metamorphosis
- Igneous rocks - formed when magma cools and hardens

Answer:

QUESTION 67

Which of the following is a large body of water that is surrounded on all sides by land?

    A. river

    B. ocean

    C. lake

    D. pond

Answer:

QUESTION 68

Food Chain: grass ---> bug ---> frog ---> owl ---> hawk

In which part of the food chain is the greatest amount of energy transferred?

    A. from owl to hawk

    B. from bug to frog

    C. from grass to bug

    D. from grass to hawk

Answer:

QUESTION 69

Which of the following best describes the function of adenosine triphosphate (ATP) in a cell?

    A. ATP transfer energy within the cell

    B. ATP collects water

    C. ATP collets waste

    D. ATP controls the amount of energy within the body

Answer:

QUESTION 70

Which of the following best describes how a virus causes an individual to develop common cold?

    A. removes healthy energy from body system

    B. invades the host cell to reproduce

    C. protects healthy bacteria

    D. allows toxins to enter the body system

Answer:

QUESTION 71

The Ring of Fire refers to the volcanoes that are:

    A. located in Africa

    B. located in Americas

    C. located in hot spots

    D. located around the borders of the Pacific Ocean

Answer:

QUESTION 72

Which of the following is the best reason for why the Sun and the Moon appear to move across the sky?

    A. the rotation of the solar system
    B. the rotation of the Earth
    C. the rotation of the Sun
    D. the rotation of the Moon

Answer:

QUESTION 73

Which of the following sources give plants the carbon dioxide needed for photosynthesis?

    A. water
    B. air
    C. sun
    D. light

Answer:

QUESTION 74

Which of the following is the best way to introduce playwriting in theater?

    A. having students write a play while watching a documentary
    B. write a letter to a play writer
    C. watch a video showing basic of playwriting
    D. show examples of play write

Answer:

QUESTION 75

What is the purpose of art exhibits and reproductions?

    A. support communities

    B. collaborate closely together

    C. show art is meaningful to communication

    D. compare work with peers

Answer:

Correct Exam Answers - Test 1

Question Number	Correct Answer	Question Number	Correct Answer	Question Number	Correct Answer	Question Number	Correct Answer
1	c	21	A	41	B	61	A
2	d	22	B	42	A	62	A
3	d	23	C	43	A	63	D
4	c	24	D	44	B	64	D
5	A	25	D	45	B	65	B
6	B	26	D	46	A	66	D
7	B	27	D	47	B	67	C
8	C	28	C	48	D	68	C
9	C	29	B	49	D	69	A
10	A	30	D	50	B	70	B
11	D	31	C	51	A	71	D
12	D	32	B	52	D	72	B
13	B	33	D	53	A	73	B
14	C	34	D	54	A	74	D
15	B	35	B	55	B	75	C
16	B	36	D	56	D		
17	A	37	C	57	B		
18	B	38	B	58	B		
19	C	39	A	59	B		
20	D	40	D	60	B		

NOTE: Getting approximately 80% of the questions correct increases chances of obtaining passing score on the real exam. This varies from different states and university programs.

This page is intentionally left blank.

Practice Exam 1 – Questions and Explanations

QUESTION 1

Mark has a writing assignment due in 5 days. In order to complete the assignment, he plans to write 15 pages during one day and writes 5 pages each remaining day as he proofreads. How many pages does Mark plan to write?

    A. 20
    B. 30
    C. 35
    D. 40

Answer: C

Explanation: Mark plans to write for a total of 5 days. On the first day he writes 15 pages, and on the following four days, he writes 5 pages. Two methods can be used to solve for the total number of pages he plans to write:

Method 1: Knowing that he will write 5 pages for 4 days, multiply 5 by 4, and add 15 (from the first day) to get the total value.

$$15+(4\times5) = 35 \text{ pages}$$

Method 2: Simply add the following to obtain the answer:

$$15+5+5+5+5 = 35 \text{ pages}$$

QUESTION 2

The elevation h in feet as a function of time of a group of hikers as they hike in a mountain is described by h=736t+3210. The variable t is time in hours, and the function is valid when 0<t<3. Which of the following statements is the best interpretation of the number 736 in the context of this problem?

    A. The elevation of the group during the first three hours of their hike.

    B. The elevation of the group as a function of time during the first three hours of their hike.

    C. The decrease in the elevation per hour of the group during the first three hours of hiking.

    D. The increase in the elevation per hour of the group during the first three hours of hiking.

Answer: D

Explanation: The equation h=736t+3210 modeling the elevation as a function of time has the form of the equation of the line in slope-intercept form y=mx+b. The variable m is the slope, and the variable b is the initial elevation. The variable m is equal to 736. The variable t is time in hours. The equation describes the elevation in feet. Therefore, the 736 is the increase in elevation per hour during the first three hours of the group's hike. It is an increase because the slope is positive.

QUESTION 3

$$-3x + 15 < 6$$

Which of the following values of x are solutions of the inequality above?

    A. 0.75

    B. 2.89

    C. 2.21

    D. 3.14

Answer: D

Explanation: The following steps are to solve the inequality:

Step 1: Subtract 15 both sides

$$-3x + 15 - 15 < 6 - 15$$
$$-3x < -9$$

Step 2: Divide both sides by -3. Multiplying and dividing inequalities by negative number requires flipping the inequality sign.

$$\frac{-3x}{-3} < \frac{-9}{-3}$$
$$x > 3$$

All choices greater than 3 are the answers, which is 3.14.

QUESTION 4

If $\dfrac{3}{x-4} = \dfrac{5}{y}$ where $y \neq 0$ and $x \neq 4$, what is y in terms of x?

    A. $y = 2x - 10$

    B. $y = \dfrac{5}{2}x + 6$

    C. $y = \dfrac{5}{3}x - \dfrac{20}{3}$

    D. $y = \dfrac{7}{3}x + \dfrac{10}{3}$

Answer: C

Explanation: Solve the equation for y.

$$\frac{3}{x-4} = \frac{5}{y}$$

$$3y = 5(x-4)$$

$$3y = 5x - 20$$

$$y = \frac{5x - 20}{3}$$

$$y = \frac{5}{3}x - \frac{20}{3}$$

QUESTION 5

Kyle jogs at least 20 minutes, and then he works out for an hour and ten minutes. What is the minimum amount of time in minutes he uses to complete his physical activities?

    A. 90 minutes

    B. 100 minutes

    C. 130 minutes

    D. 150 minutes

Answer: A

Explanation: Add the minutes for Kyle's physical activities. Kyle jogs for 20 minutes and works out for an hour and ten minutes, which is equivalent to 70 minutes. Adding 20 minutes and 70 minutes gives a total minimum of 90 minutes.

QUESTION 6

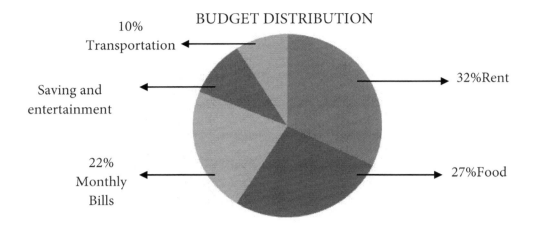

BUDGET DISTRIBUTION

10%
Transportation

32%Rent

Saving and
entertainment

22%
Monthly
Bills

27%Food

The graph above shows the percent of Mary's monthly budget distributed into her more important expenses. What percent of her monthly budget can she use for saving and entertainment?

    A. 8%

    B. 9%

    C. 10%

    D. 11%

Answer: B

Explanation: The question is asking to figure out the monthly budget Mary uses for saving and entertainment. From the chart, add up all the percents and subtract the result from 100 %

$$10\%+22\%+32\%+27\% = 91\%$$
$$100\%-91\% = 9\%$$

QUESTION 7

Tom buys a package that contains 432 marbles. If he seeks to distribute packs of 15 marbles to his classmates, what is the total number of complete packs that he can make?

    A. 22

    B. 28

    C. 29

    D. 30

Answer: B

Explanation: In order to determine the number of complete packs Tom can make, divide the total number of marbles (432) by the number marbles he wants in each pack (15). For this problem, the interest is in the whole number as the question is asking for the complete number of packages.

$$432 \div 15 = 28.8$$

Therefore, the final answer is 28 packs.

QUESTION 8

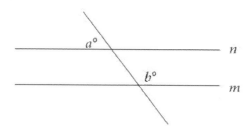

In the figure above, line n and line m are parallel, and b = 3a. What is the value of a?

    A. 25°

    B. 35°

    C. 45°

    D. 55°

Answer: C

Explanation: The sum of the measures of supplementary angle is 180°. That is a+b = 180. The question states that b=3a. Substituting for b results in 4a=180, giving a=45°.

QUESTION 9

If $\frac{1}{5}x - \frac{1}{4}y = 10$, what is the value of $4x - 5y$?

    A. 100
    B. 160
    C. 200
    D. 240

Answer: C

Explanation: Rearrange the original equation, so the left hand side is equal to $4x - 5y$.

$$\frac{1}{5}x - \frac{1}{4}y = 10$$

First, multiply both sides by 5.

$$x - \frac{5}{4}y = 50$$

Second, multiply both sides by 4.

$$4x - 5y = 200$$

QUESTION 10

Month	Miles Driven
January	2600
February	3000
March	3200
April	2400
May	1800
June	
July	3400
August	3200
September	2500
October	2700
November	1900
December	2200

The table above shows the approximate number of miles driven by Bill during each month in the past year. How many miles did Bill drive during June if the arithmetic mean of the miles driven for the entire year was 2600?

A. 2300 miles

B. 2400 miles

C. 2500 miles

D. 2550 miles

Answer: A

Explanation: The mean value is given, so multiply the mean (2600) by the number of months in the table, which is 12.

$$2,600 \times 12 = 31,200 \text{ miles}$$

The total number of miles driven must equal 31,200. To determine the missing value for June, add up all the miles provided in the table, which will be 28,900 miles. The last step would be to subtract 28,900 from 31,200 to obtain the final answer of 2,300 miles.

QUESTION 11

Printers A and B work together to complete an assigned job. Printer A completes this job in 8 hours. Both printers working together complete the job in 6 hours. How many hours does it take for Printer B to complete the job if it was working alone?

    A. 16
    B. 18
    C. 20
    D. 24

Answer: D

Explanation: Printer A completes a job at rate of 1 job per 8 hours.

$$A = \frac{1 \text{ job}}{8 \text{ hours}}$$

Both printers together complete the job at a rate of 1 job every 6 hours.

$$A + B = \frac{1 \text{ job}}{6 \text{ hours}}$$

Combine the expression above and solve for B.

$$\frac{1}{8} + B = \frac{1}{6}$$

$$B = \frac{1}{6} - \frac{1}{8} = \frac{1}{24}$$

This indicates that printer B completes 1 job every 24 hours.

QUESTION 12

In a map displaying the freeway system, 1 inch is represented by 200 miles. How many inches on the map represent a freeway of 2,460 miles of length?

    A. 9.6

    B. 9.8

    C. 10.8

    D. 12.3

Answer: D

Explanation: This is a proportion problem requiring cross multiplication to solve for the missing value.

$$\frac{1 \text{ inch}}{200 \text{ miles}} = \frac{x \text{ inches}}{2,460 \text{ miles}}$$

After cross multiplying:

$$2,460 = 200 \times x$$

Divide both sides by 200, giving the final answer:

$$\frac{2,460}{200} = \frac{200 \times x}{200}$$

$$x = 12.3 \text{ inches}$$

QUESTION 13

A machine can perform 40 identical tasks in 4 hours. At this rate, what is the minimum number of machines that should be assigned to complete 90 of the tasks within 2 hours?

   A. 4
   B. 5
   C. 7
   D. 8

Answer: B

Explanation: The key is to find out how many machines are needed to do a certain number of tasks in 2 hours. If one machine can do 40 tasks in 4 hours, in 2 hours it will complete 20 tasks. So, if there are two machines, that is 40 tasks, three machines is 60 tasks, four machines is 80 tasks, and five machines is 100 tasks. Using four machines is not an option as the goal is to do 90 tasks. The best option is B.

QUESTION 14

A certain doctor earns n dollars for each individual she consults with plus x dollars for every 15 minutes the doctor consults. If in a certain week she works 14 hours and supports 15 individuals, how much does she earn for that week, in dollars?

   A. $14n + 15$

   B. $15n \times 15x + 15$

   C. $15n + \frac{14 \times 60}{15} x$

   D. $15x + \frac{14 \times 60}{15} n$

Answer: C

Explanation: 15 individuals saw the doctor for which she will receive a total of 15n dollars. She worked 14 hours, which is equal to (14×60) minutes. For every 15 minutes, the doctor gets paid x dollars, so divide $(14 \times 60)/15$ and multiply by x to get the total amount of dollars the doctor received for working.

QUESTION 15

156, 176, 198, x, 165

The range calculated for the above data is 45. Determine the missing value, x?

    A. 111
    B. 153
    C. 178
    D. 200

Answer: B

Explanation: The range between the highest and the lowest known values is 198 – 156 = 42. Therefore, the highest value has to be increased by 3 or the lowest value decreased by 3. The numbers become 201 and 153. Answer option B is 153, which is the answer.

QUESTION 16

$$\sqrt{(8 \times 72)} =$$

    A. 20
    B. 24
    C. 36
    D. 48

Answer: B

Explanation: 8×72 gives 576. The square root of 576 is 24.

QUESTION 17

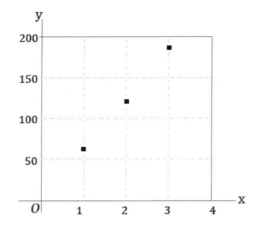

What relationship can be represented by the data points in the graph above?

    A. hours and minutes
    B. meters and inches
    C. meters and yards
    D. weeks and months

Answer: A

Explanation: Look at the data points (1, 60), (2, 120), and (3, 180). The relationship shown is for hours and minutes. 1 hour = 60 minutes, 2 hours = 120 minutes, and 3 hours = 180 minutes.

QUESTION 18

If x-2y=0 and -2x+y=2, then 3x-3y=

    A. -4
    B. -2
    C. 0
    D. 3

Answer: B

Explanation: To find the value of 3x-3y, subtract the equations given. Remember to distribute the negative sign, which will change all the signs in the second equation.

$$x-2y = 0$$
$$\underline{-1(-2x+y) = -1(2)}$$
$$= 3x - 3y = -2$$

NOTE: The answer to this problem can be reached by solving for x and y, which is a long process. Doing long calculations and processes during the exam might be indication there is a hidden trick to solve the problem.

QUESTION 19

The figure is a parallelogram. If 65 < k < 80, select all the following that could be the value of n?

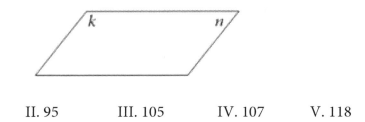

I. 89　　　　II. 95　　　　III. 105　　　　IV. 107　　　　V. 118

A. I and III
B. II and IV
C. III and IV
D. II and V

Answer: C

Explanation: The problem gives a range for k. Using the lower limit of the range, 65, the value of n can be found by: 180 – 65 = 115. Using the upper limit of the range, 80, the value of n can be found by: 180 – 80 = 100. The answer has to be between 100 and 115. The answers are 105 and 107.

QUESTION 20

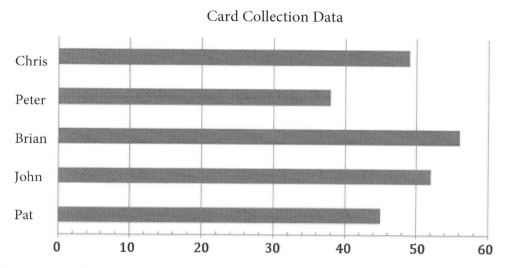

Card Collection Data

Five kids meet to play a trading card game. The number of cards each kid had initially is shown in the graph above. After the game, Pat had 28; John had 45; Brian had 52; and Chris had 63. How many cards does Peter have after the game?

   A. 10
   B. 28
   C. 38
   D. 52

Answer: D

Explanation: The question asks to find the number of cards Peter has after the game. Add all number of cards from the chart (45 + 52 + 56 + 38 +49 = 240). The total is 240. Then, subtract the amount of cards the other people have after the game.

$$240-28-45-52-63 = 52$$

QUESTION 21

The following formula is the volume of a sphere:

$$\text{Volume of Sphere} = \frac{4}{3} \times \pi \times r^3$$

What is the volume in cubic inches of spherical balloon that has a diameter of 8 inches?

    A. $\frac{256}{3}\pi$

    B. $\frac{512}{3}\pi$

    C. $\frac{64}{3}\pi$

    D. $\frac{2048}{3}\pi$

Answer: A

Explanation: The following formula is the volume of a sphere:

$$\text{Volume of Sphere} = \frac{4}{3} \times \pi \times r^3$$

Knowing the diameter gives the value of the radius, which is 4. The answer choices are in terms of π, so leave that in the answer without performing the numerical multiplication.

$$\text{Volume of Sphere} = \frac{4}{3} \times \pi \times 4^3$$
$$\text{Volume of Sphere} = \frac{4}{3} \times \pi \times 64$$
$$\text{Volume of Sphere} = \frac{256}{3} \times \pi$$

QUESTION 22

Brand A sells erasers in packages of 4, while Brand B sells erasers in packages of 3. If Donna buys 12 packages of Brand A, then how many packages of Brand B does she have to buy to get the same quantity?

A. 18
B. 16
C. 14
D. 12

Answer: B

Explanation: Donna brought 12 packages of Brand A, which contained 4 erasers, so multiply 12 and 4, which gives her a total of 48 erasers. Brand B contains 3 erasers. To obtain the number of Brand B packages she needs to buy to obtain 48 erasers, divide 48 by 3, which gives 16 packages.

QUESTION 23

Which of the following numbers has a square that is less than itself?

A. -3
B. 0
C. 0.3
D. 3

Answer: C

Explanation: Numbers less than 1 and greater than 0 provide a square that is less than itself. Square of 0 is 0. Square of numbers larger than 1 provide a square that is larger than itself. Numbers given by $0<x<1$ are the only numbers that have squares less than themselves.

QUESTION 24

0.376544376544376544376544...

In the decimal number above, the first six digits to the right of the decimal point repeat indefinitely in the same order. What is the 326th digit to the right of the decimal point?

    A. 4
    B. 5
    C. 6
    D. 7

Answer: D

Explanation: The first six digits are of a pattern that continues. To determine the 326th digit, divide 326 by 6, which gives 54 with remainder of 2. With the remainder being 2, go to the second number of the pattern to obtain the answer, which is 7.

QUESTION 25

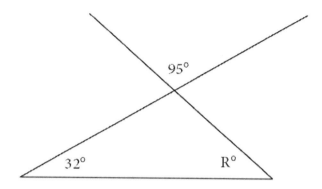

From the figure above, determine the value of the angle, R.

    A. 32°
    B. 37°
    C. 39°
    D. 53°

Answer: D

Explanation: The sum of angles of a triangle is 180°. One of the angle values is directly given as 32°. The other value can be obtained from the information of 95° as the opposite angle would be the same. All values of the angle for the triangle are known except for one, which can be solved by:

$$180° - 95° - 32° = 53°$$

QUESTION 26

In a classroom, 19 kids have at least one brother and 13 kids have at least one sister. Of the kids who have a brother or a sister, 8 have both a brother and a sister. If there are 35 kids in the class, how many kids do NOT have any siblings?

    A. 15
    B. 12
    C. 14
    D. 11

Answer: D

Explanation: To determine the number of kids that do not have siblings, determine the total number of kids that do have brothers and sisters. From the problem, 19 kids have brothers and 13 kids have sisters, so total number of kids that have brothers and sisters is 32. However, 8 kids have both brothers and sisters, so subtract 8 from 32 to prevent double counting of those who have both brothers and sisters. The total number of kids that have a brother or a sister is 24 kids. To determine the number of kids that do not have siblings, subtract 24 from the total number of kids in class (35 kids), which gives the final answer of 11 kids.

QUESTION 27

If x is divisible by 8, then it is divisible by 6

The above statement is false, if x equals:

A. 6
B. 14
C. 48
D. 64

Answer: D

Explanation: First, eliminate all the answer choices that are not divisible by 8, which eliminates A and B. To make the statement false, find an answer choice that is not divisible by 6, which is D.

QUESTION 28

Use the chart below for the next three questions.

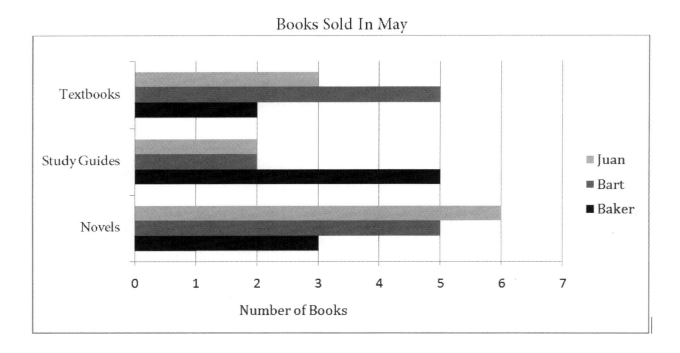

Which type of book was sold the most?

    A. Textbooks
    B. Study Guides
    C. Novels
    D. Textbooks and Novels

Answer: C

Explanation: When calculating the total number of each type of book that was sold, novels had the highest number of 14. Textbooks ranked second with 10 sold, while study guides ranked last with only 9 sold.

QUESTION 29

The above chart shows the different types of books sold by Juan, Bart, and Baker in the month of May. What is the mean of the books sold by the three individuals?

    A. 10
    B. 11
    C. 12
    D. 13

Answer: B

Explanation: To determine the mean value, add all the number of books sold.
$$3+5+2+2+5+5+6+5+3=33$$
Divide 33 by 3 as there are three individuals, giving the answer of 11.

QUESTION 30

Of the three types of books, which of the three books contains the value of the mode?

    I.   Textbooks
    II.   Study Guides
    III.   Novels

    A. II only
    B. I and II
    C. I and III
    D. I, II, and III

Answer: D

Explanation: The mode for the data set is 2 and 5 as these numbers appear the most. The number 2 appears in the textbooks sold and the number 2 appears twice in the study guides sold. The number 5 appears in all three study guides. Therefore, all three books contain the value of the mode.

QUESTION 31

Bill is ten years older than his sister. If Bill was twenty-five years of age in 1983, in what year was he born?

A. 1948
B. 1953
C. 1958
D. 1963

Answer: C

Explanation: The first sentence of this problem is not needed as that is extra information. If Bill was 25 years old in 1983, subtract 25 from 1983 to obtain his birth year.

$$1983-25=1958$$

QUESTION 32

The following are the scores Todd made on his exams during the Spring Semester: 90, 90, 90, 77, 75, 100, 84, 82 and 71. The instructor drops the two lowest scores and replaces those scores with the two highest scores. What is the average of Todd's scores?

A. 84.33
B. 89.22
C. 99.22
D. 90.00

Answer: B

Explanation: The two lowest scores are 71 and 75, and the two highest scores are 100 and 90. The two lowest scores need to be replaced with the two highest scores. The following is the new score list:

$$90, 90, 90, 77, 90, 100, 84, 82 \text{ and } 100$$

To calculate the mean, add up all the scores to obtain the total value.

$$90 + 90 + 90 + 77 + 90 + 100 + 84 + 82 + 100 = 803$$

Divide the result obtained by the total number of scores, which is 9.

$$\frac{803}{9} = 89.22$$

QUESTION 33

John had two grocery bags, and they were weighed to the nearest kilogram. The bags weighed 33kg and 43kg. If the combined weight was W kg, which is true?

    A. $76.5 \leq W \leq 77$
    B. $72 \leq W \leq 73$
    C. $74.5 \leq W \leq 75.5$
    D. $75.5 \leq W \leq 76.5$

Answer: D

Explanation: The combined weight can be found by adding the individual bag weights, which would be 43 + 33 = 76. From the choices provided, the only valid statement is D because the number 76 falls in that interval.

QUESTION 34

The width of Marty's backyard is 43.2 feet and the length is 32.1 feet. What is the area of the rectangular shaped backyard?

    A. 150.5 feet^2
    B. 160.6 feet^2
    C. 150.6 feet^2
    D. 1386.72 feet^2

Answer: D

Explanation: To obtain the area of a rectangle, multiply the length by the width.

$$43.2 \times 32.1 = 1386.72$$

QUESTION 35

Of the following, which is/are greater than 1.25?

I. 125%   II. 3/2   III. 150%   IV. 2/3   V. 12.5%

A. I and II
B. II and III
C. II and IV
D. III and IV

Answer: B

Explanation: Convert all options to decimals format.

- 125% = 1.25
- 3/2 = 1.5
- 150% = 1.5
- 2/3 = 0.6667
- 12.5% = 0.125

3/2 and 150% are the only two greater than 1.25. The question states only greater than and not greater than or equal to, so 125% is not an answer.

QUESTION 36

If x is a real number and an integer and completes the solution $x^4 = 16$, which statement is true?

A. x is less than 4
B. x is greater than 4
C. x is less than 2
D. x = 2

Answer: D

Explanation: Perform the following operation:

$$2^4 = 2 \times 2 \times 2 \times 2 = 16$$

QUESTION 37

Sports Day Teams

Number of Teams	Students Per Team
4	3
2	8
6	2

From the chart, how many total students are there?

    A. 12
    B. 13
    C. 40
    D. 44

Answer: C

Explanation: To obtain the total number of students, multiply the number of teams by the number of students.

$$4\times3 = 12$$
$$2\times8 = 16$$
$$6\times2 = 12$$

Total number of students can be determined by adding the above results.

$$12+16+12 = 40$$

QUESTION 38

If the area of a triangle is $A = \frac{1}{2}\times b\times h$, then what would be the area of two triangles of the same size and shape?

    A. $2\times h$
    B. $b\times h$
    C. $2\times b\times h$
    D. b^2h^2

Answer: B

Explanation: If the area of one triangle is $A = (\frac{1}{2})\times b\times h$, then the area of two triangles can be found by multiplying by 2.

$$2 \times \left(\frac{1}{2}\right) \times b\times h = b\times h$$

QUESTION 39

What is the main reason why no vaccine shots have been created for common cold?

    A. too many causes of common cold to develop vaccine
    B. common cold has to run its course
    C. because it is a virus
    D. it contains bacteria

Answer: A

Explanation: Nearly 250 viruses can cause the common cold, so to develop vaccine shots will be difficult. Options B and C are correct, but those options are not the main reason, which the question is asking for.

QUESTION 40

Which of the following is not considered a high cloud?

    A. cirrus
    B. cirrostratus
    C. cirrocumulus
    D. cumulus

Answer: D

Explanation: Cirrus, cirrostratus, and cirrocumulus clouds are all considered high cloud. Cumulus cloud is considered a low cloud.

QUESTION 41

What is average height of an American male?

    A. 60 inches
    B. 70 inches
    C. 80 inches
    D. 90 inches

Answer: B

Explanation: The average American men height is 69.7 inches. The best answer is Option B.

QUESTION 42

Which of the following is the best option to weight a person?

    A. scale using lbs
    B. scale using grams
    C. dropped weight scale
    D. body mass scale

Answer: A

Explanation: Option C and D do not make sense in weighing a person. Option B is good option, but the best way to measure weight is lbs.

QUESTION 43

Indigenous individuals living in the tropical regions of the world had contribution to modern science. Which practice is the most significant influence to modern science?

    A. using medicinal plants to treat illnesses

    B. developing the compass

    C. devising a plan to clean ocean water for daily use

    D. improving framing practices to better the nutrients levels of sand

Answer: A

Explanation: Indigenous people had to use medicinal plants to treat illnesses. The practices used by the Indigenous people carried to modern science medicine.

QUESTION 44

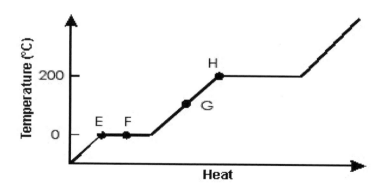

Mr. Clayton is conducting a mini experiment in which a sample of frozen water is being heated over a bunsen burner. He has documented the temperature and the heat during the experiment. The results are shown in the graph above, which shows a curve as it is heated from solid to liquid to gas phases. The beaker contains a mixture of the sample in both the solid and liquid phase at point _____.

    A. E
    B. F
    C. G
    D. H

Answer: B

Explanation: The question is asking for when the mixture is both in the solid and liquid phase, which is indicated by point F. From 0 to point E, the phase is solid. After that, the horizontal line is the phase change, which is the state of solid and liquid.

QUESTION 45

Marine organisms play a significant part in the existence of fossils mostly because

    A. the pressure of the ocean water destroys animal life resulting in fossils
    B. sedimentary rocks' material exist at the bottom of the ocean
    C. the high water pressure results in fossils
    D. the energy in the fossils are a result of dead marine organism

Answer: B

Explanation: Marine organisms live under water, and sedimentary rocks' material exist at the bottom of the ocean.

QUESTION 46

Which of the following is the process in which rocks are broken down into smaller fragments by the atmosphere and other factors in the environment?

    A. weathering
    B. osmosis
    C. decartelization
    D. erosion

Answer: A

Explanation: Weather is the process in which rocks are broken down into smaller fragments by the atmosphere and other factors in the environment.

QUESTION 47

When individuals are constantly involved in resistance weight training, they are likely to benefit the body by:

- A. decreasing chances of heart disease
- B. increasing bone density
- C. increasing blood flow
- D. decreasing joint dismemberment

Answer: B

Explanation: Resistance weight training applies active stress on the skeletal system, which leads to an increase in the density of long bones. This occurs because of an increase in mineral deposition into the bone matrix.

QUESTION 48

Which of the following medium results in sound to travel the fastest?

- A. air
- B. light
- C. water
- D. wire

Answer: D

Explanation: Sound can travel faster through wire than any other option provided. Sound waves travel fastest through a solid material.

QUESTION 49

Which of the following is not true about arthropod?

- A. Arthropods have a segmented body, a tough exoskeleton, and jointed appendages.
- B. Arthropods are surrounded by a tough external covering, or exoskeleton.
- C. Arthropods include insects, crabs, centipedes, and spiders.
- D. Appendages are structures that do not extend from the body wall.

Answer: D

Explanation: All options are true except for Option D. Appendages are jointed structures that extend from the body wall.

QUESTION 50

An early childhood teacher is having students drop common objects into a water table. The teacher has the student document which item floats or sinks. Afterwards, a discussion is held on the common properties for objects that sink and float. Which of the following concepts is best introduced with this activity?

    A. water properties
    B. density
    C. volume
    D. mass

Answer: B

Explanation: Density is mass per unit volume. Heavier objects will sink while lighter objects may float. The teacher is attempting to teach the concept of density.

QUESTION 51

A cumulus cloud starts to form in a warm air mass that is ascending rapidly through a slightly cooler air mass. Of the following, which is likely the most logical cause of condensation in the warm air mass?

    A. a reduction in temperature caused by the reduction in atmospheric pressure
    B. a reduction in temperature caused by the heat transfer of two masses
    C. an increase in temperature resulting in the increase in dew point
    D. an increase in relative humidity caused on the increase in water content

Answer: A

Explanation: Cumulus clouds are puffy clouds that sometimes look like pieces of floating cotton. A cumulus cloud starts to form in a warm air mass that is ascending rapidly through a slightly cooler air mass. The reason for this is a reduction in temperature caused by reduction in atmospheric pressure.

QUESTION 52

Of the following, which is considered a vertebrate?

    A. jellyfish
    B. butterfly
    C. earthworm
    D. hummingbird

Answer: D.

Explanation: Hummingbird is vertebrate. Vertebrates are the most advanced organisms on Earth. A vertebrate is an animal that has a backbone and a skeleton.

QUESTION 53

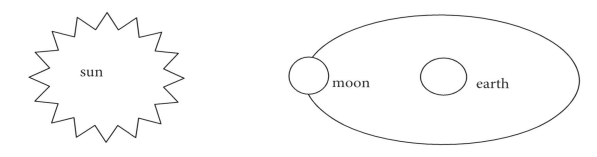

The above illustration is an example of:

    A. a solar eclipse
    B. a lunar eclipse
    C. a moon depiction
    D. earth configuration

Answer: A

Explanation: A solar eclipse is a type of eclipse that occurs when the Moon passes between the Sun and Earth. A lunar eclipse happens when the Moon passes directly behind the Earth into its umbra.

QUESTION 54

Data obtained for the variables x and y are collected during an experiment and given below.

X	4	8	16	20	24	28
Y	.05	.19	.33	.47	.61	.75

Which of the following best describes the relationship between x and y?

    A. linear
    B. inverse
    C. constant
    D. no relationship

Answer: A

Explanation: For every x, the value is increased by 4. With that, for every y, the value is increased by 0.14. This is a linear relationship.

QUESTION 55

An area is most likely to experience _____ the day after a cold front passes.

    A. severe weather
    B. lower temperature
    C. cloud cover
    D. drought conditions

Answer: B

Explanation: The air behind a cold front is obviously colder and drier than the air ahead of it. After a cold front passes through, temperatures will drop.

QUESTION 56

Which of the following is one of the layers of Earth's atmosphere?

A. Corona
B. Biosphere
C. Nebula
D. Stratosphere

Answer: D

Explanation: Troposphere, Stratosphere, Mesosphere, Thermosphere, Ionosphere, and Exosphere are the layers of the Earth's atmosphere.

QUESTION 57

I.   provides the energy to move the body
II.   provides a rigid frame that supports many organs of the body
III. provides oxygen storage for the body during times of strenuous exertion

Of the above, which of the following correctly states the function(s) of the human skeletal system?

A. I only
B. II only
C. I and II
D. II and III

Answer: B

Explanation: The human skeletal system provides a rigid frame that supports many organs of the body.

QUESTION 58

A storm in high plains moves toward the Mid-West. What most likely causes the storms to strengthen?

    A. air pressure

    B. clash of cold, dry air from the north

    C. wind from the west

    D. wind from the east

Answer: B

Explanation: Cold, dry air is a cause of storms gaining strength.

QUESTION 59

    I.   A burner on a propane stove is lighted to heat water.

    II.   Boiling water is poured through a filter containing ground coffee.

Which of the following steps in making a cup of coffee involves a physical change in the matter?

    A. I only

    B. II only

    C. I and II

    D. None of the above

Answer: B

Explanation: A burner on a propane stove is lighted to heat water will result in physical change in the matter. Physical changes can be reversed.

QUESTION 60

I.   A basketball thrown across a field will fall in an arc to the ground.

II. A hockey puck gliding on ice will continue moving until friction reduces the speed.

Which of the following statements illustrates Newton's first law of motion?

  A. I only
  B. II only
  C. I and II
  D. none of the above

Answer: B

Explanation: Newton's first law of motion states an object at rest remains at rest and an object in motion remains in motion with the same speed and in the same direction unless acted upon by an unbalanced force. The unbalanced force is friction, and the hockey puck moves until acted upon by the unbalanced force.

QUESTION 61

Which of the following is a renewable source of energy?

  A. biomass
  B. gas
  C. coal
  D. oil

Answer: A

Explanation: Biomass is a renewable source of energy as it is a resource which can be used repeatedly because it is replaced naturally.

QUESTION 62

Water changing forms of energy due to the environment is an example of which of the following?

   A. dew on grass
   B. frost on windshield
   C. puddle in road
   D. rain cloud

Answer: A

Explanation: On a cool morning, droplets of dew cover the grass. Air is made of a mixture of various gases, including water vapor. Some of the water vapor condenses the cool grass and forms drops of liquid water.

QUESTION 63

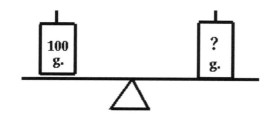

Which of the following will balance the balance scale?

   A. 10
   B. 20
   C. 50
   D. 100

Answer: D

Explanation: Clearly shown from the image above, 100 g will result an equal balance.

QUESTION 64

Smoking, poor nutrition, inactive, and excessive sleeping are examples of what form of health risk factors?

    A. physical fitness
    B. biological factors
    C. inherited factors
    D. behavioral factors

Answer: D

Explanation: All these factors are individuals choices, so the risk factors are behavioral related.

QUESTION 65

    I.   transformations
    II.   translocations
    III. additions
    IV.   losses

From above, which of the following is the correct order of how soil is formed?

    A. II, I, III, IV
    B. III, IV, II, I
    C. I, II, III, IV
    D. I, IV, III, II

Answer: B

Explanation: The following is the order of how soil is formed: additions, losses, translocations, and transformations.

QUESTION 66

Which of the following correct defines how the major rocks are formed?

A.
- Sedimentary rocks – formed when magma cools and hardens
- Metamorphic rocks – formed under the surface of the earth from the metamorphosis
- Igneous rocks - formed from particles of sand, shells, and other fragments of material

B.
- Sedimentary rocks – formed under the surface of the earth from the metamorphosis
- Metamorphic rocks – formed from particles of sand, shells, and other fragments of material
- Igneous rocks - formed when magma cools and hardens

C.
- Sedimentary rocks – formed from particles of sand, shells, and other fragments of material
- Metamorphic rocks – formed when magma cools and hardens
- Igneous rocks - formed under the surface of the earth from the metamorphosis

D.
- Sedimentary rocks – formed from particles of sand, shells, and other fragments of material
- Metamorphic rocks – formed under the surface of the earth from the metamorphosis
- Igneous rocks - formed when magma cools and hardens

Answer: D

Explanation: Option D correctly defines how sedimentary, metamorphic, and igneous rocks are formed.

QUESTION 67

Which of the following is a large body of water that is surrounded on all sides by land?

    A. river

    B. ocean

    C. lake

    D. pond

Answer: C

Explanation: A lake is a large body of water that is surrounded on all sides by land. An ocean is a vast body of salt water that surrounds a continent. A river is a large, flowing body of water that empties into a sea or an ocean. A pond is also surrounded on all sides by land and is typically smaller than a lake.

QUESTION 68

Food Chain: grass ---> bug ---> frog ---> owl ---> hawk

In which part of the food chain is the greatest amount of energy transferred?

    A. from owl to hawk

    B. from bug to frog

    C. from grass to bug

    D. from grass to hawk

Answer: C

Explanation: The grass has the most energy as it is the first item listed. As the energy is transferred to the bug, the bug receives the most energy.

QUESTION 69

Which of the following best describes the function of adenosine triphosphate (ATP) in a cell?

    A. ATP transfer energy within the cell

    B. ATP collects water

    C. ATP collets waste

    D. ATP controls the amount of energy within the body

Answer: A

Explanation: The role of adenosine triphosphate (ATP) is to transfer energy within a cell.

QUESTION 70

Which of the following best describes how a virus causes an individual to develop common cold?

    A. removes healthy energy from body system

    B. invades the host cell to reproduce

    C. protects healthy bacteria

    D. allows toxins to enter the body system

Answer: B

Explanation: Viruses invade host cells, which use the host cell to reproduce. This causes a person to develop the symptoms of a common cold.

QUESTION 71

The Ring of Fire refers to the volcanoes that are:

    A. located in Africa

    B. located in Americas

    C. located in hot spots

    D. located around the borders of the Pacific Ocean

Answer: D

Explanation: The Ring of Fire refers to the volcanoes that are located around the borders of the Pacific Ocean.

QUESTION 72

Which of the following is the best reason for why the Sun and the Moon appear to move across the sky?

    A. the rotation of the solar system
    B. the rotation of the Earth
    C. the rotation of the Sun
    D. the rotation of the Moon

Answer: B

Explanation: The apparent movements of the Sun and the Moon across the sky are caused by the rotation of the Earth on its axis.

QUESTION 73

Which of the following sources give plants the carbon dioxide needed for photosynthesis?

    A. water
    B. air
    C. sun
    D. light

Answer: B

Explanation: Air is the source that gives plants the carbon dioxide needed for photosynthesis.

QUESTION 74

Which of the following is the best way to introduce playwriting in theater?

    A. having students write a play while watching a documentary
    B. write a letter to a play writer
    C. watch a video showing basic of playwriting
    D. show examples of play write

Answer: D

Explanation: Having students write about playwrite is not going to be the best way to introduce playwriting in theater. Watching a video is not as effective as showing examples, so the answer is D.

QUESTION 75

What is the purpose of art exhibits and reproductions?

    A. support communities
    B. collaborate closely together
    C. show art is meaningful to communication
    D. compare work with peers

Answer: C

Explanation: Art is a form of communication. Displaying art exhibits and reproductions is way to show the importance of the art along with communicating the message associated with the art.

Practice Test 2

This page is intentionally left blank.

Exam Answer Sheet Test 2

Below is an optional answer sheet to use to document answers.

Question Number	Selected Answer	Question Number	Selected Answer	Question Number	Selected Answer	Question Number	Selected Answer
1		21		41		61	
2		22		42		62	
3		23		43		63	
4		24		44		64	
5		25		45		65	
6		26		46		66	
7		27		47		67	
8		28		48		68	
9		29		49		69	
10		30		50		70	
11		31		51		71	
12		32		52		72	
13		33		53		73	
14		34		54		74	
15		35		55		75	
16		36		56			
17		37		57			
18		38		58			
19		39		59			
20		40		60			

This page is intentionally left blank.

Practice Exam 2 - Questions

QUESTION 1

Meg is a teacher at a local elementary school. She is doing an activity with sticky notes. She has students put the number of individuals living in their homes on the sticky notes and place it on a horizontal line. Then, they take the sticky notes and arrange them from the most number of individuals living in homes to least number of individuals living in homes. What concept is the teacher aiming to support the students in understanding?

    A. mean
    B. mode
    C. medium
    D. range

Answer:

QUESTION 2

Kate has 4 shirts, 7 pants, and 3 hats. If each day she wears exactly 1 shirt, 1 pant, and 1 hat, what is the maximum number of days she can go without repeating a particular combination?

    A. 12
    B. 21
    C. 28
    D. 84

Answer:

QUESTION 3

In the number 3010, the value represented by the digit 1 is what fraction of the value represented by the digit 3.

    A. $\dfrac{1}{3000}$

    B. $\dfrac{1}{300}$

    C. $\dfrac{1}{30}$

    D. $\dfrac{1}{3}$

Answer:

QUESTION 4

The normal price of a desk is $120 and the normal price of a printer is $30. An electronics store has a discount that offers a 30% discount on the printer when the desk is purchased at the regular price. What is the total cost of the desk and the printer at the discount price?

    A. 150
    B. 141
    C. 129
    D. 109

Answer:

QUESTION 5

If $\frac{3}{a+3} = \frac{2}{y}$ where y≠0 and a≠-3, what is y in terms of a?

    A. $y=2a+6$

    B. $y=\frac{3}{2}a+6$

    C. $y=\frac{2}{3}a-2$

    D. $y=\frac{2}{3}a+2$

Answer:

QUESTION 6

$$d=\frac{e^2+f^2}{ef}$$

(e and f are positive numbers)

What is the corresponding change in the value of d if the values of e and f are each multiplied by 100?

    A. It will be multiplied by 100.
    B. It will be multiplied by 1000.
    C. It will be divided by 100.
    D. It will remain unchanged.

Answer:

QUESTION 7

$$\{11, D, 23, E, F, 68, 75\}$$

If half of the range of the increasing series is equal to its median, what is the median of the series?

A. 22
B. 31
C. 32
D. 43

Answer:

QUESTION 8

If Jake flips a coin twice, what is the probability that at least one head will be thrown?

A. 0.25
B. 0.45
C. 0.50
D. 0.75

Answer:

QUESTION 9

John's weekly income consists of his hourly wages and a $50 weekly allowance given to him by his father. Maria's weekly income consists of her hourly wages and a weekly allowance given to her by her father. John earns $10 an hour and Maria earns $12 an hour. If they each work for 10 hours in one week, how much weekly allowance does Maria's father need to give her, so both Maria and John earn the same income in that week?

A. $20
B. $30
C. $50
D. $120

Answer:

QUESTION 10

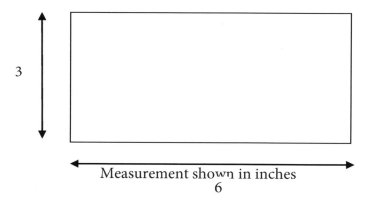

3

Measurement shown in inches
6

In the diagram above, the numbers are rounded to the nearest whole numbers. Which of the following is a possible value of the area of the rectangle?

    A. 8 square inches
    B. 14 square inches
    C. 19 square inches
    D. 20 square inches

Answer:

QUESTION 11

Each of the following is equivalent to 25% of 60 except:

    A. $25 \times \frac{25}{100}$

    B. 0.25×60

    C. $\frac{1}{4} \times 60$

    D. $\frac{60 \times 75}{300}$

Answer:

QUESTION 12

A second grade teacher is having each student stand on a large sheet of one inch graph paper. Each student's partner outlines the student's foot by tracing around it. Afterwards, the students then count the number of squares enclosing the outline. Which of the following is math concept is best being exposed to the student with this activity?

A. area
B. perimeter
C. graphing
D. proportion

Answer:

QUESTION 13

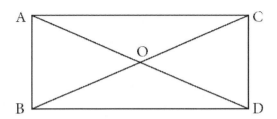

In the diagram, line CB and line DA intersect at O. If BC = -4x – 2 and OD = 2x + 5, what is the value of line AD?

A. 2
B. 4
C. 6
D. 8

Answer:

QUESTION 14

In Barry's company, the ratio of the number of male employees to the number of female employees is exactly 2 to 3. Which of the following could be the total number of employees in the company?

    A. 88
    B. 96
    C. 100
    D. 112

Answer:

QUESTION 15

A machine can perform 40 identical tasks in 4 hours. At this rate, what is the minimum number of machines that should be assigned to complete 90 of the tasks within 2 hours?

    A. 4
    B. 5
    C. 7
    D. 8

Answer:

QUESTION 16

A certain doctor earns n dollars for each individual she consults with, plus x dollars for every 15 minutes the doctor consults. If in a certain week she works 14 hours and supports 15 individuals, how much does she earn for that week, in dollars?

    A. $14n + 15$
    B. $15n \times 15x + 15$
    C. $15n + \frac{14 \times 60}{15} x$
    D. $15x + \frac{14 \times 60}{15} n$

Answer:

QUESTION 17

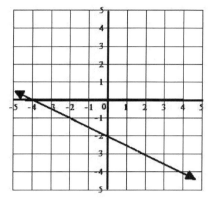

Which of the following equations represents the line above?

    A. $y = (2/4)x + 2$

    B. $y = (1/2)x - 2$

    C. $y = -(2/4)x - 2$

    D. $y = -(1/2)x + 2$

Answer:

QUESTION 18

Two sisters decide to start a business. They will make and deliver balloons for special occasions. It will cost them $59.99 to buy the machine to fill the balloons with air. Based on their calculation, it will cost them $3.00 to buy the balloon and ribbon needed to make each balloon. Which of the following expressions could be used to model the total cost for producing b balloons?

    A. $3.00b + $59.99

    B. $54.99b

    C. $3.00b - $59.99

    D. $59.99b + $3.00b

Answer:

QUESTION 19

$$y = \frac{x+6}{x-6}$$

What are the domain and range for the relation above?

    A. Domain = {all real numbers}, Range = {all real numbers}
    B. Domain = {all real numbers ≠ 6}, Range = {all real numbers}
    C. Domain = {all real numbers ≠ −6}, Range = {all real numbers}
    D. Domain = {all real numbers}, Range = {all real numbers ≠ 6}

Answer:

QUESTION 20

The following steps are taken to solve the inequality:

Step 1: $3(x+6) \leq 5(x+2)$

Step 2: $3x+18 \leq 5x+2$

Step 3: $3x-5x \leq -18+2$

Step 4: $-2x \leq -16$

Step 5: $x \leq -8$

Step 6: $x \geq -8$

Which of the following step(s) did the student make a mistake?

    A. Step 2
    B. Step 3
    C. Step 6
    D. Step 2 and 5

Answer:

QUESTION 21

Jake has two rectangles, C and D, are similar. Rectangle C has a length of 100 inches and a width of 50 inches. The area of rectangle D is 200 square inches. What is its perimeter for rectangle D?

A. 20 inches
B. 40 inches
C. 60 inches
D. 80 inches

Answer:

QUESTION 22

Given $f(x) = x^2 + x - 3$, find $f(-3)$,

A. 3
B. 6
C. 9
D. 15

Answer:

QUESTION 23

At Blake's Pizza, there are 4 types of cheeses, 5 meat options, and 4 veggie options. How many pizza combinations are possible?

A. 13
B. 16
C. 60
D. 80

Answer:

QUESTION 24

Use the table below to answer the question that follows.

Section	Total Number of Questions	Number of Questions Correctly Answered
Pre-Algebra	18	16
Algebra	12	11
Geometry	20	18

The above table shows the performance of a student on a math exam with three sections. What percent of the questions on the entire exam did the student answer incorrectly?

    A. 10%
    B. 30%
    C. 55%
    D. 75%

Answer:

QUESTION 25

Mr. Martin needs to order rope for his afterschool physical education class of 24 students. The rope cost $1.50 per feet. Each student will get a piece of rope that is 4 feet 7 inches long. What is the total cost of rope Mr. Martin needs to order for his class?

    A. $36
    B. $90
    C. $110
    D. $165

Answer:

QUESTION 26

A doctor works 2 days per week at a hospital that is open Monday through Friday. If the workdays are randomly assigned, what is the probability that the doctor will work on Monday and Wednesday?

   A. 2/10
   B. 1/10
   C. ½
   D. 2/7

Answer:

QUESTION 27

Use the diagram below to answer the question that follows.

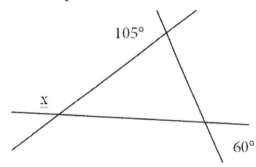

In the above diagram, the three straight lines intersect to form a triangle. What is the measure of angle x?

   A. 135
   B. 120
   C. 75
   D. 65

Answer:

QUESTION 28

During a quality control check, a production facility found that 6% of the parts it produces are not aligned with the specification. The factory recently completed an order for 143,000 parts. What is the best estimate of how many of the parts from the order may be out of specification?

    A. 3,800
    B. 8,600
    C. 9,000
    D. 11,000

Answer:

QUESTION 29

Two squares are shown above. The gray square length is 4 inches. The white square is 2 inches wider on each side. What is the perimeter of the white square?

    A. 8
    B. 16
    C. 24
    D. 36

Answer:

QUESTION 30

Jason uses 1 box of bird food every 5 days to feed the birds outside the church. Approximately, how many boxes of bird food does Jason use per month?

A. 4
B. 5
C. 6
D. 7

Answer:

QUESTION 31

Mary has a bag of fruits. The bag contains 20 apples, 17 grape fruits, 12 bananas, and 8 peaches. Mary randomly takes one apple from the bag and gives it to her friend. What is the probability that she will next take an apple or a banana?

A. 19/56
B. 31/57
C. 31/56
D. 228/3136

Answer:

QUESTION 32

An elementary teacher has three packages of paper. One paper package contains 34 blue pages, another package contains 40 green pages, and the third package contains 70 white pages. If the teacher divides all the pages equally among 22 students, how many pages will each student receive?

    A. 5

    B. 6

    C. 7

    D. 8

Answer:

QUESTION 33

At the beginning of math class, half of the students go to the gym. One hour later, half of the remaining students go to the cafeteria. If there are 9 students remaining in the math class, how many students were originally in the class?

    A. 9

    B. 18

    C. 24

    D. 36

Answer:

QUESTION 34

A car rental company charges $10.00 per day plus tax for a basic automobile. The tax rate is 8.25%, and the company also charges a one-time untaxed fee of $75.00. If a person rents a basic automobile for x days and spends $120 dollars in gas, which of the following represents the amount of money spent by this person?

    A. $1.0825(10.00x)+195$

    B. $(10.00+8.25x)+195$

    C. $1.0825(10.00x+195)$

    D. $8.25(10.00x)+195$

QUESTION 35

The school policy is to have one bus driver and each bus cannot have more than 20 individuals (not included bus driver) total. The school policy is also to have two adults accompany every 15 students on school trips. With a total of 180 students, how many total seats will be needed for a school trip?

A. 192
B. 204
C. 214
D. 215

Answer:

QUESTION 36

What was the total number of games sold?

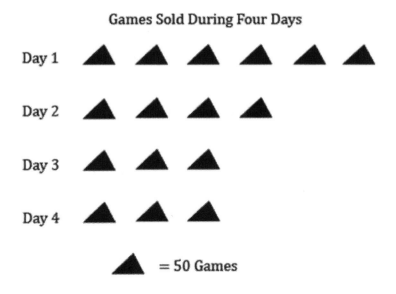

Games Sold During Four Days

A. 600
B. 650
C. 700
D. 800

Answer:

QUESTION 37

The following graph indicates the number of computers sold each week at a store. Estimate the number of computers sold in a monthly period. A month is approximated to be four weeks.

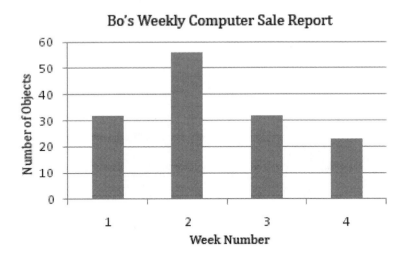

Bo's Weekly Computer Sale Report

A. 83
B. 97
C. 123
D. 143

Answer:

QUESTION 38

The following chart indicates the grade distribution in a college math class with 58 students. About how many students passed the class if at least a C grade is needed to accomplish this?

Percentage of Grades

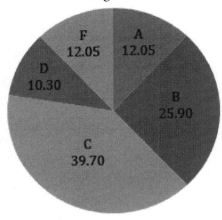

A. 48 students
B. 45 students
C. 42 students
D. 40 students

Answer:

QUESTION 39

Which of the following is the main cause of tide?

A. wind
B. gravity
C. ocean currents
D. rain

Answer:

QUESTION 40

In Northern hemisphere, surface currents always move water _____.

    A. clockwise
    B. counter-clockwise
    C. parallel
    D. horizontally

Answer:

QUESTION 41

The continental crust is the thickest beneath which of the following?

    A. mountains
    B. oceans
    C. plains
    D. forest

Answer:

QUESTION 42

_____ is the planet that could float on water due to its low density.

    A. Venus
    B. Mars
    C. Saturn
    D. Jupiter

Answer:

QUESTION 43

Of the following, which position of a roller coaster has the greatest amount of potential energy?

A. at the bottom of a hill
B. at the middle of a hill
C. as it travels up a hill
D. when at resting point

Answer:

QUESTION 44

RNA is produced from DNA in the process of _____.

A. synthesis
B. replication
C. transcription
D. translation

Answer:

QUESTION 45

Which of the following would be the best use for a material that reflects almost all light?

A. window
B. mirror
C. light paper
D. black paper

Answer:

QUESTION 46

Which of the following best describes mutation?

    A. a change that is inherited

    B. a change that is developed

    C. a change impacted later in life

    D. a controlling factor in plant growth

Answer:

QUESTION 47

Which of the following is incorrectly described?

    A. circulatory system – breathing system

    B. digestive system – food processing system

    C. nervous system - transports messages

    D. muscular system – movement of the body

Answer:

QUESTION 48

How does the human body maintain a constant temperature?

    A. homeostasis

    B. isotherm process

    C. release of energy

    D. intake of protein

Answer:

QUESTION 49

A fourth grade student sees a puddle of water on the sidewalk when she travels to school. As she travels back home, the puddle of water is gone. What happened to the water in the puddle?

    A. it disappears
    B. it freezes
    C. it condenses
    D. it evaporates

Answer:

QUESTION 50

In the winter, the pond begins to freeze, causing the ducks to leave the pond to migrate to warmer climates. The ducks migrate because they have

    A. difficulty finding food
    B. too many enemies
    C. have to lay eggs near water
    D. too few places to hibernate

Answer:

QUESTION 51

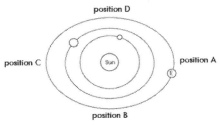

Where will the Earth (indicated by E) be in six months?

    A. near position D
    B. near position C
    C. near position B
    D. near position A

Answer:

QUESTION 52

Which is the first step in a design process?

- A. test the possible solutions
- B. revise the solution
- C. describe the problem
- D. identify possible solutions

Answer:

QUESTION 53

The two students want classmates to repeat the investigation so that they can compare results.

When repeating an investigation, what should the students communicate so that the results may be compared?

- A. origin of the materials for model telephones
- B. materials and steps used in the investigation
- C. conclusions about results from first investigation
- D. communicate hypothesis

Answer:

QUESTION 54

In a lesson, the students will study how water changes from liquid to gas.

Materials: electric heating coil, beaker and thermometer

Procedure:

A. Pour one liter of water into the beaker.
B. Place the thermometer in the water.
C. Record the temperature of the water.
D. Place the beaker on the heating coil.
E. Turn on the heating coil.
F. Record the temperature of the water every minute for 10 minutes.

Of the following, what can be done to ensure safety in this experiment?

I.   slowly pour water into beaker
II.   keep close distance from hot heating coil
III.   ensure outside of the glass beaker is not wet

A. I only
B. I and II
C. I and III
D. I, II, and III

Answer:

QUESTION 55

Which weather observation is likely just before a heavy snowstorm?

A. clear sky
B. thick gray clouds
C. small white clouds
D. warm temperature

Answer:

QUESTION 56

Butterflies obtain food from the flowers of a plant. They also lay their eggs on the leaves of the plant. As the caterpillars develop, they eat the leaves. Plants benefit from the butterflies as the butterflies

A. help add nutrients to the nectar of the flowers
B. help pollinate flowers so that seeds can form
C. help the plant grow larger flowers
D. help grow the plants leaves

Answer:

QUESTION 57

A student took two ice cubes from the freezer and put them in a glass of freshly squeezed kiwi fruit juice. After 15 minutes, the student tried to take the ice cubes out of the juice, but there were gone. What type of change took place?

A. chemical, because the ice cubes became a new substance
B. physical, because the ice cubes evaporated
C. chemical, because the ice cubes' energy became heat
D. physical, because the ice cubes changed into liquid

Answer:

QUESTION 58

Soil in an empty field blows away during a strong wind. Which activity slows the erosion of this field over time?

    A. building fence
    B. watering
    C. plowing
    D. planting grass

Answer:

QUESTION 59

What makes a plant bend toward the light?

    A. phototropism
    B. photosynthesis
    C. cellular respiration
    D. convection

Answer:

QUESTION 60

Engaging the entire family in a healthy eating plan is most likely the best approach in which of the following?

    A. Supporting elementary students to eating healthy.
    B. Supporting an adolescent in losing weight.
    C. Teaching kids on importance of eating healthy.
    D. Supporting state curriculum of teaching healthy eating at home.

Answer:

QUESTION 61

In which of the following can sound waves not travel in?

    A. a vacuum.

    B. air

    C. water

    D. building

Answer:

QUESTION 62

An object moves in the direction in which the force is applied. The previous statement is an example of

    A. potential energy

    B. power

    C. work

    D. inertia

Answer:

QUESTION 63

Which scientific law states that a body accelerates in the direction of the net force applied?

    A. Newton's first law

    B. Newton's second law

    C. Boyle's law

    D. Faraday's law

Answer:

QUESTION 64

    I.   to respond readily to instructions

    II.   to follow rules, codes, and safety practices

    III.   to work with other students to ensure learning

    IV.   to warm up and recover from exercise

Which of the following are ways to teach students on ensuring safe practices are being implemented in physical education classrooms?

  A. I and II
  B. II and III
  C. I, II, and IV
  D. II, III, and IV

Answer:

QUESTION 65

What is the difference between weight and mass?

  A. mass is the amount of matter in an object while weight is measurement of the gravitational pull on an object
  B. mass is the amount of particles in an object while weight is measurement of the gravitational pull away an object
  C. mass is the measure of the total object while measurement is the measure of the object with gravitational pull
  D. mass is the amount of matter in while weight is measurement of the dimension of the object

Answer:

QUESTION 66

In design, which of the following is common challenge of complex systems?

    A. closed loop system

    B. many parts and connections

    C. open loop system

    D. increase cost of designing

Answer:

QUESTION 67

For an unordered system to become more ordered, which of the following is required?

    A. increase in pressure

    B. expenditure of energy

    C. increase in the size of the system

    D. increase in heat

Answer:

QUESTION 68

A pitcher plant traps insects in a pitcher-shaped leaf from which the insect is unable to escape. Which of the following best describes the reason for this strategy?

    A. allow the plant more carbohydrates

    B. attract more insects

    C. help the plant survive

    D. dissuade insect predation

Answer:

QUESTION 69

A basketball rolls down an incline and then goes on to a flat, smooth surface until it stops. Which of the following best explains why the ball came to a halt?

    A. The weight of the ball caused it to stop.

    B. The frictional forces overcame the ball's inertia.

    C. There was no gravity force on the flat surface.

    D. The potential energy was gone when ball was on the flat surface.

Answer:

QUESTION 70

Which of the following is the main cause of the sun having high temperatures?

    A. nuclear fusion reactions

    B. nuclear fission reactions

    C. chemical reactions

    D. angular momentum

Answer:

QUESTION 71

While working on a class physics experiment, Juan dropped a glass test tube filled with an unknown liquid. What should Juan do first?

    A. clean up the spill

    B. inform the teacher

    C. walk away

    D. put on gloves

Answer:

QUESTION 72

Which of the following biogeochemical cycles is most impacted by the erosion of limestone?

    A. the water cycle

    B. the carbon cycle

    C. the oxygen cycle

    D. none of the above

Answer:

QUESTION 73

    I.   rust forming on an outcrop of iron-rich rock

    II.   limestone dissolving

    III.   melting water

Of the above, which of the following is/are shows of chemical weathering involving oxygen?

    A. I only

    B. I and II

    C. I and III

    D. I, II, and III

Answer:

QUESTION 74

What type of dance involves individuals holding hands in a circle?

    A. chain dance

    B. folk dance

    C. ballroom dance

    D. modern dance

Answer:

QUESTION 75

What is the term for light and dark areas on paintings?

A. chiaroscuro
B. value
C. color
D. illusion

Answer:

This page is intentionally left blank.

Correct Exam Answers - Test 2

Question Number	Correct Answer	Question Number	Correct Answer	Question Number	Correct Answer	Question Number	Correct Answer
1	C	21	C	41	A	61	A
2	D	22	A	42	C	62	C
3	B	23	D	43	B	63	B
4	B	24	A	44	C	64	C
5	D	25	D	45	B	65	A
6	D	26	B	46	A	66	B
7	C	27	A	47	A	67	B
8	D	28	B	48	A	68	B
9	B	29	C	49	C	69	B
10	B	30	C	50	A	70	A
11	A	31	C	51	B	71	B
12	A	32	B	52	C	72	B
13	B	33	D	53	B	73	A
14	C	34	A	54	C	74	A
15	B	35	D	55	B	75	A
16	C	36	D	56	B		
17	C	37	D	57	D		
18	A	38	B	58	D		
19	B	39	B	59	A		
20	D	40	A	60	B		

NOTE: Getting approximately 80% of the questions correct increases chances of obtaining passing score on the real exam. This varies from different states and university programs.

This page is intentionally left blank.

Practice Exam 2 – Questions and Explanations

QUESTION 1

Meg is a teacher at a local elementary school. She is doing an activity with sticky notes. She has students put the number of individuals living in their homes on the sticky notes and place it on a horizontal line. Then, they take the sticky notes and arrange them from the most number of individuals living in homes to least number of individuals living in homes. What concept is the teacher aiming to support the students in understanding?

A. mean
B. mode
C. medium
D. range

Answer: C

Explanation: The teacher is having the students put the numbers in order from greatest to least. For mean, mode, and range, the need to put the numbers in order is not always necessary. Typically, for medium, the numbers are put in order to see which number is in the middle.

QUESTION 2

Kate has 4 shirts, 7 pants, and 3 hats. If each day she wears exactly 1 shirt, 1 pant, and 1 hat, what is the maximum number of days she can go without repeating a particular combination?
A. 12
B. 21
C. 28
D. 84

Answer: D

Explanation: Kate has 4 shirts, 7 pants, and 3 hats. To find the combination without repeating, multiply 4 shirts, 7 pants, and 3 hats to get 84.

QUESTION 3

In the number 3010, the value represented by the digit 1 is what fraction of the value represented by the digit 3.

A. $\dfrac{1}{3000}$

B. $\dfrac{1}{300}$

C. $\dfrac{1}{30}$

D. $\dfrac{1}{3}$

Answer: B

Explanation: This problem requires understanding the place value system and using fractions. To find the value represented by the digits, the place value system is used.

$$3010$$

(3 = thousands, 0 = hundreds, 1 = tens, 0 = ones)

This represents that the number $3010 = (3 \times 1000) + (0 \times 100) + (1 \times 10) + (0 \times 1)$. The value for the digit 3 is 3000, and the value for the digit 1 is 10. Using fractions,

$$\frac{\text{value represented by the digit 1}}{\text{value represented by digit 3}} = \frac{10}{3000} = \frac{1}{300}$$

QUESTION 4

The normal price of a desk is $120 and the normal price of a printer is $30. An electronics store has a discount that offers a 30% discount on the printer when the desk is purchased at the normal price. What is the total cost of the desk and the printer at the discount price?

A. 150

B. 141

C. 129

D. 109

Answer: B

Explanation: With the 30% discount, the printer will cost $9 less ($30 × 0.30 = $9). The printer will cost $21. Adding the $21 to the price of the desk gives total of $141.

QUESTION 5

If $\frac{3}{a+3}=\frac{2}{y}$ where $y\neq0$ and $a\neq-3$, what is y in terms of a?

   A. $y=2a+6$

   B. $y=\frac{3}{2}a+6$

   C. $y=\frac{2}{3}a-2$

   D. $y=\frac{2}{3}a+2$

Answer: D

Explanation: Solve the equation for y.

$$\frac{3}{a+3}=\frac{2}{y}$$

Cross-multiply on both sides.

$$3y=2(a+3)$$

Distribute on the right hand side of the equation.

$$3y=2a+6$$

Divide both sides by 3.

$$\frac{3y}{3}=\frac{2a+6}{3}$$

$$y=\frac{2}{3}a+\frac{6}{3}$$

$$y=\frac{2}{3}a+2$$

QUESTION 6

$$d = \frac{e^2 + f^2}{ef}$$

(e and f are positive numbers)

What is the corresponding change in the value of d if the values of e and f are each multiplied by 100?

    A. It will be multiplied by 100.
    B. It will be multiplied by 1000.
    C. It will be divided by 100.
    D. It will remain unchanged.

Answer: D

Explanation: Multiplying e and f by 100 has the same effect on the numerator and denominator. This allows for the effect to cancel, resulting in the same expression as originally given.

$$d = \frac{(100e)^2 + (100f)^2}{(100e)(100f)} = \frac{100^2[e^2 + f^2]}{(100)(100)[ef]} = \frac{e^2 + f^2}{ef}$$

QUESTION 7

$$\{11, D, 23, E, F, 68, 75\}$$

If half of the range of the increasing series is equal to its median, what is the median of the series?

    A. 22
    B. 31
    C. 32
    D. 43

Answer: C

Explanation: Don't get confused with all the variables. Range is the difference between the smallest term and largest term (75 − 11 = 64). The question states that the median is equal to half of the range, so the answer is 32.

QUESTION 8

If Jake flips a coin twice, what is the probability that at least one head will be thrown?

    A. 0.25

    B. 0.45

    C. 0.50

    D. 0.75

Answer: D

Explanation: The desired outcomes are HH, HT, or TH. Possible outcomes are HH, HT, TH, or TT. Of the 4 possible outcomes, 3 are desired, so the probability is $\frac{3}{4}$=0.75.

QUESTION 9

John's weekly income consists of his hourly wages and a $50 weekly allowance given to him by his father. Maria's weekly income consists of her hourly wages and a weekly allowance given to her by her father. John earns $10 an hour and Maria earns $12 an hour. If they each work for 10 hours in one week, how much weekly allowance does Maria's father need to give her, so both Maria and John earn the same income in that week?

    A. $20

    B. $30

    C. $50

    D. $120

Answer: B

Explanation: To solve this problem, John's weekly income needs to be calculated. He earns $50 from his father and $100 from his work (10 hours × $10/hr); this adds to a total weekly income of $150. The next step is to model Maria's income as a function of her allowance and hours worked. This model is a linear equation equal to 12h + b; where h is the hours worked and b is her allowance. Since the problem states Maria's income should be equal to John's income, the linear equation is set equal to $150. The problems also states she works for 10 hours, so h will equal to 10 in the equation. These two substitutions result in 12×10 + b = 150, which can be solved for b = $30.

QUESTION 10

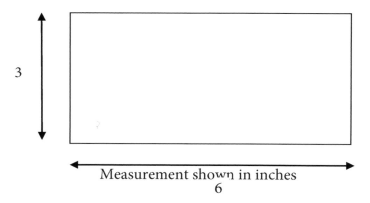

3

Measurement shown in inches

6

In the diagram above, the numbers are rounded to the nearest whole numbers. Which of the following is a possible value of the area of the rectangle?

    A. 8 square inches
    B. 14 square inches
    C. 19 square inches
    D. 20 square inches

Answer: B

Explanation: As indicated in the question, the numbers are rounded to the nearest whole numbers. Based on rounding rules, the smallest possible values for the width is 2.5 inches. Anything under 2.5 inches will result in rounding down to 2. Based on rounding rules, the smallest possible values for the length is 5.5 inches. Anything under 5.5 inches will result in rounding down to 5. With the formula for area being length times width, the area is 5.5 times 2.5, which gives 13.75. The closest answer is 14.

QUESTION 11

Each of the following is equivalent to 25% of 60 except:

A. $25 \times \frac{25}{100}$

B. 0.25×60

C. $\frac{1}{4} \times 60$

D. $\frac{60 \times 75}{300}$

Answer: A

Explanation: 25% can be written as 0.25 and $\frac{1}{4}$, and so B and C are eliminated. In D, notice that 75/300 equals ¼, which be written as 25%.

QUESTION 12

A second grade teacher is having each student stand on a large sheet of one inch graph paper. Each student's partner outlines the student's foot by tracing around it. Afterwards, the students then count the number of squares enclosing the outline. Which of the following is math concept is best being exposed to the student with this activity?

A. area
B. perimeter
C. graphing
D. proportion

Answer: A

Explanation: The student is counting the squares that are enclosed in the outline, so the student is being exposed to the concept of area.

QUESTION 13

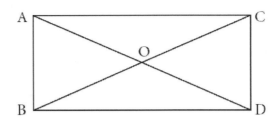

In the diagram, line CB and line DA intersect at O. If BC = -4x – 2 and OD = 2x + 5, what is the value of line AD?

    A. 2
    B. 4
    C. 6
    D. 8

Answer: B

Explanation: Line BC must equal line AD as the lines intersect at O.
$$BC = AD \text{ (Equation 1)}$$
The question only gives equation for OD, so use the following relationship:
$$AD = 2 \times OD \text{ (Equation 2)}$$
Insert Equation 1 into Equation 2,
$$BC = 2 \times OD$$
$$BC = -4x – 2 \text{ and } OD = 2x + 5$$
$$-4x – 2 = 2 \times (2x + 5) \text{ (Equation 3)}$$
Solve for x in Equation 3,
$$-4x – 2 = 4x + 10$$
$$-8x = 12$$
$$x = -(3/2)$$
With Equation 2 and OD = 2x + 5, insert –(3/2) for x
$$AD = 2 (2x + 5)$$
$$AD = 4x + 10$$
$$AD = 4(-3/2) + 10$$
$$AD = -(12/2) + 10$$
$$AD = -6 + 10$$
$$AD = 4$$

QUESTION 14

In Barry's company, the ratio of the number of male employees to the number of female employees is exactly 2 to 3. Which of the following could be the total number of employees in the company?

- A. 88
- B. 96
- C. 100
- D. 112

Answer: C

Explanation: One approach to solving is to use the answer choices. With the ratio, "male employees to the number of female employees is exactly 2 to 3", the ratio for total male employees to total employees can be obtained as 2/5 (Note: 5 is obtained from adding 2 and 3). Using proportions,

$$\frac{2}{5} = \frac{x}{100} \text{ (x is the number of male employees)}$$

Solving for x,

$$2 \times 100 = 5x$$
$$200 = 5x$$
$$x = 40$$

With there being 40 male employees, there are 60 female employees, so establishing a fraction with male employees on the numerator and female employees on the denominator,

$$\frac{40}{60} = \frac{4}{6} = \frac{2}{3}$$

The ratio of the male employees to the number of female of 2/3 is obtained.

QUESTION 15

A machine can perform 40 identical tasks in 4 hours. At this rate, what is the minimum number of machines that should be assigned to complete 90 of the tasks within 2 hours?

    A. 4
    B. 5
    C. 7
    D. 8

Answer: B

Explanation: The key is to find out how many machines are needed to do a certain number of tasks in 2 hours. If one machine can do 40 tasks in 4 hours, in 2 hours it will complete 20 tasks. So, if there are two machines, that is 40 tasks, three is 60 tasks, four is 80 tasks, and five is 100 tasks. Using four machines is not an option as the goal is to do 90 tasks.

QUESTION 16

A certain doctor earns n dollars for each individual she consults with plus x dollars for every 15 minutes the doctor consults. If in a certain week she works 14 hours and supports 15 individuals, how much does she earn for that week, in dollars?

    A. $14n + 15$
    B. $15n \times 15x + 15$
    C. $15n + \frac{14 \times 60}{15}x$
    D. $15x + \frac{14 \times 60}{15}n$

Answer: C

Explanation: 15 individuals saw the doctor for which she will receive a total of 15n dollars. She worked 14 hours, which is equal to (14 × 60) minutes. For every 15 minutes, the doctor gets paid x dollars, so divide (14 × 60)/15 and multiply by x to get the total amount of dollars the doctor received for working.

QUESTION 17

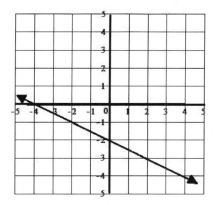

Which of the following equations represents the line above?

    A. y = (2/4)x + 2
    B. y = (1/2)x – 2
    C. y = -(2/4)x – 2
    D. y = -(1/2)x + 2

Answer: C

Explanation: Using the equation y = mx + b, with m being the slope and b being the y=intercept, y-intercept is shown on the graph as -2. The slope is -2/4 (go up two units and four units to the left; negative sign is due to going left). The equation is y = -(2/4)x – 2.

QUESTION 18

Two sisters decide to start a business. They will make and deliver balloons for special occasions. It will cost them $59.99 to buy the machine to fill the balloons with air. Based on their calculation, it will cost them $3.00 to buy the balloon and ribbon needed to make each balloon. Which of the following expressions could be used to model the total cost for producing b balloons?

    A. $3.00b + $59.99
    B. $54.99b
    C. $3.00b - $59.99
    D. $59.99b + $3.00b

Answer: A

Explanation: The start-up cost is $59.99. The cost for each balloon is $3.00, so it will cost $3.00b to produce b balloons. Add 3.00b and $59.99 to get $3.00b + $59.99.

QUESTION 19

$$y = \frac{x+6}{x-6}$$

What are the domain and range for the relation above?

    A. Domain = {all real numbers}, Range = {all real numbers}
    B. Domain = {all real numbers ≠ 6}, Range = {all real numbers}
    C. Domain = {all real numbers ≠ −6}, Range = {all real numbers}
    D. Domain = {all real numbers}, Range = {all real numbers ≠ 6}

Answer: B

Explanation: Domain is all x values, and x cannot equal 6 as the denominator will be 0. The answer is B. No restrictions exists for the range.

QUESTION 20

The following steps are taken to solve the inequality:

$$\text{Step 1: } 3(x+6) \leq 5(x+2)$$
$$\text{Step 2: } 3x+18 \leq 5x+2$$
$$\text{Step 3: } 3x-5x \leq -18+2$$
$$\text{Step 4: } -2x \leq -16$$
$$\text{Step 5: } x \leq -8$$
$$\text{Step 6: } x \geq -8$$

Which of the following step(s) did the student do incorrectly?

A. Step 2
B. Step 3
C. Step 6
D. Step 2 and 5

Answer: D

Explanation: In Step 2, the five needs to be distributed to the 2. Dividing a negative number by a negative results in the negative sign turning into a positive sign. In Step 5, it should be 8 instead of -8.

QUESTION 21

Jake has two rectangles, C and D, are similar. Rectangle C has a length of 100 inches and a width of 50 inches. The area of rectangle D is 200 square inches. What is its perimeter for rectangle D?

A. 20 inches
B. 40 inches
C. 60 inches
D. 80 inches

Answer: C

Explanation: Rectangle C and D are similar, so the length and width of rectangle D must be proportional to the length and width of rectangle C. Moreover, the product of the width and length of rectangle D must equal 200 square inches. Taking the length of rectangle D as 20 inches and width as 10 inches gives an area of 200 square inches. The length and width also satisfy the condition that rectangle C and D are similar; multiplying 20 inches and 10 inches each by 5 results in 100 inches and 50 inches, which indicates similarity with Rectangle C. The perimeter of rectangle D is 20 + 10 + 20 + 10 = 60

QUESTION 22

Given $f(x)=x^2+x-3$, find $f(-3)$,

    A. 3
    B. 6
    C. 9
    D. 15

Answer: A

Explanation: Insert -3 in the function and solve,

$$f(x)=(-3)^2+(-3)-3=9-3-3=3$$

QUESTION 23

At Blake's Pizza, there are 4 types of cheeses, 5 meat options, and 4 veggie options. How many pizza combinations are possible?

    A. 13
    B. 16
    C. 60
    D. 80

Answer: D

Explanation: Multiplying 4 types of cheese, 5 meat options, and 4 veggie options, gives an answer of 80.

QUESTION 24

Use the table below to answer the question that follows.

Section	Total Number of Questions	Number of Questions Correctly Answered
Pre-Algebra	18	16
Algebra	12	11
Geometry	20	18

The above table shows the performance of a student on a math exam with three sections. What percent of the questions on the entire exam did the student answer incorrectly?

A. 10%
B. 30%
C. 55%
D. 75%

Answer: A

Explanation: From the table, obtain the total number of questions and total number of correctly answered questions.

- Total number of questions: 18 + 12 + 20 = 50
- Total number of questions correctly answered: 16 + 11 + 18 = 45

The question asks for the percent of questions the student answered incorrectly. To obtain that value, first subtract 45 from 50, giving 5 questions answered incorrectly. Then, divide 5 by 50 (total questions) and reduce the fraction by 5, giving:

$$\frac{5}{50} \div \frac{5}{5} = \frac{1}{10} = 0.10 = 10\%$$

QUESTION 25

Mr. Martin needs to order rope for his afterschool physical education class of 24 students. The rope cost $1.50 per feet. Each student will get a piece of rope that is 4 feet 7 inches long. What is the total cost of rope Mr. Martin needs to order for his class?

    A. $36
    B. $90
    C. $110
    D. $165

Answer: D

Explanation: Convert 4 feet 7 inches to the unit of inches only by:
$$(4 \times 12) + 7 = 55 \text{ inches}$$
Each student will need 55 inches of rope, and there are total 24 students, so the total length can be obtained by multiplying:
$$55 \times 24 = 1320 \text{ inches}$$
The question gives the cost per foot, so convert the 1320 inches to feet by:
$$\frac{1320}{12} = 110 \text{ feet}$$
The question states 1 foot cost $1.50, so the total cost of the rope is:
$$110 \times \$1.50 = \$165$$

QUESTION 26

A doctor works 2 days per week at a hospital that is open Monday through Friday. If the workdays are randomly assigned, what is the probability that the doctor will work on Monday and Wednesday?

    A. 2/10
    B. 1/10
    C. ½
    D. 2/7

Answer: B

Explanation: Total possible outcome is 5 (Monday, Tuesday, Wednesday, Thursday, and Friday). Probability of Monday and Wednesday being selected is 2/5. Let's say that Monday was selected, then the doctor has four days left and one possible outcome left (Wednesday), so probability is 1/4. Multiple 2/5 and 1/4,

$$\frac{2}{5} \times \frac{1}{4} = \frac{2}{20} \div \frac{2}{2} = \frac{1}{10}$$

In probability questions, if the word "and" is used, it likely is an indication to multiply.

QUESTION 27

Use the diagram below to answer the question that follows.

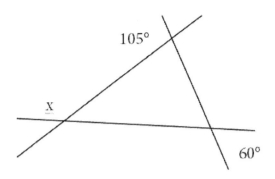

In the above diagram, the three straight lines intersect to form a triangle. What is the measure of angle x?

    A. 135
    B. 120
    C. 75
    D. 65

Answer: A

Explanation: The key is to find the angles associated with the triangle. The angle of straight line is 180 degrees. The angle opposite of intersection is equal to each other, such as 60 degrees and 75 degrees.

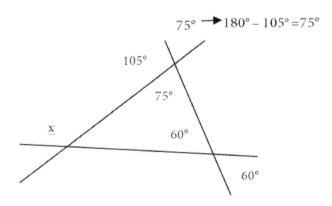

A triangle has 180 degrees. Knowing that one angle is 75 degrees and the other is 60 degrees, the third angle is 45 degrees (180 – 75 – 60 = 45). To find x, subtract 180 degrees from 45 degrees to obtain 135 degrees.

QUESTION 28

During a quality control check, a production facility found that 6% of the parts it produces are not aligned with the specification. The factory recently completed an order for 143,000 parts. What is the best estimate of how many of the parts from the order may be out of specification?

    A. 3,800
    B. 8,600
    C. 9,000
    D. 11,000

Answer: B

Explanation: Multiplying 0.06 by 143,000 gives the answer 8,560. The best answer is 8,600.

QUESTION 29

Two squares are shown above. The gray square length is 4 inches. The white square is 2 inches wider on each side. What is the perimeter of the white square?

    A. 8
    B. 16
    C. 24
    D. 36

Answer: C

Explanation: The gray square length is 4 inches, so all sides of the square are 4 inches. The white square is 2 inches wider, so the sides are 6 inches. To obtain the perimeter add 6 + 6 + 6 + 6 = 24 inches.

QUESTION 30

Jason uses 1 box of bird food every 5 days to feed the birds outside the church. Approximately, how many boxes of bird food does Jason use per month?

    A. 4
    B. 5
    C. 6
    D. 7

Answer: C

Explanation: The maximum number of days in a month is 31 days. Divide 31 by 6 to obtain 6.2. With 30 days in a month and dividing by 5, results in 6 as the answer. With 28 days in a month and dividing by 5, gives answer of 5.6. In each of these scenarios the approximate answer results in 6.

QUESTION 31

Mary has a bag of fruits. The bag contains 20 apples, 17 grape fruits, 12 bananas, and 8 peaches. Mary randomly takes one apple from the bag and gives it to her friend. What is the probability that she will next take an apple or a banana?

    A. 19/56
    B. 31/57
    C. 31/56
    D. 228/3136

Answer: C

Explanation: The total number of fruits is 20 + 17 + 12 + 8 = 57. If Mary takes one apple, the total number of fruits remaining is 56 with only 19 apples remaining. Then, the probability of selecting an apple is 19/56, and the probability of selecting a banana is 12/56. To answer the question of "the probability that she will next take an apple or a banana" add the two probabilities to get 31/56. The use of "or" implies adding probabilities.

QUESTION 32

An elementary teacher has three packages of paper. One paper package contains 34 blue pages, another package contains 40 green pages, and the third package contains 70 white pages. If the teacher divides all the pages equally among 22 students, how many pages will each student receive?

A. 5
B. 6
C. 7
D. 8

Answer: B

Explanation: The total number of pages is 144 (34 + 40 + 70 = 144). With there being 22 students, divide 144 by 22 to obtain approximately 6.55. The question states the pages are to be divided equally among the 22 students, so the total number of pages each student will receive is 6.

QUESTION 33

At the beginning of math class, half of the students go to the gym. One hour later, half of the remaining students go to the cafeteria. If there are 9 students remaining in the math class, how many students were originally in the class?

A. 9
B. 18
C. 24
D. 36

Answer: D

Explanation: Work the problem backwards. If 9 students remain in the math class at the end, there had to be 18 students before the students went to the cafeteria. If 18 students were in the class after half students went to the gym, then the total number of students in the math class had to be 36 students. Now, work out the problem from the start. In summary, if 36 students were in the classroom, half of them went to the gym, so 18 students remained. Of those 18 students, half went to the cafeteria, so 9 students remained in the math class.

QUESTION 34

A car rental company charges $10.00 per day plus tax for a basic automobile. The tax rate is 8.25%, and the company also charges a one-time untaxed fee of $75.00. If a person rents a basic automobile for x days and spends $120 dollars in gas, which of the following represents the amount of money spent by this person?

A. 1.0825(10.00x)+195

B. (10.00+8.25x)+195

C. 1.0825(10.00x+195)

D. 8.25(10.00x)+195

Answer: A

Explanation: $10.00 is charged during x days, and this amount is taxed at a rate of 8.25%. This translates into 1.0825(10.00x). The untaxed fee of $75.00 and the amount spent in gas of $120.00 add to a total of $195. Combining 1.0825(10.00x) and $195, gives the expression 1.0825(10.00x)+195.

QUESTION 35

The school policy is to have one bus driver and each bus cannot have more than 20 individuals (not including the bus drivers) total. The school policy is also to have two adults accompany every 15 students on school trips. With a total of 180 students, how many total seats will be needed for a school trip?

A. 192
B. 204
C. 214
D. 215

Answer: D

Explanation: The question is asking for total seats needed. To obtain the number of adults needed, divide 180 by 15, which gives the answer of 12, and then multiple by 2 (as two adults are needed for every 15 students). Total adults required are 24. With 24 adults and 180 students, the total number of individuals needing a seat on buses is 204. Each bus can hold 20 individuals, so to obtain the number of total buses required, divide 204 by 20 to get 10.2. The number of bus needed is 11 to hold all 204 individuals. In regards to seats, there will be 11 bus drivers, so the total number of seats for students, adults, and bus drivers is 215.

QUESTION 36

What was the total number of games sold?

Games Sold During Four Days

Day 1

Day 2

Day 3

Day 4

= 50 Games

A. 600
B. 650
C. 700
D. 800

Answer: D

Explanation: There are 16 triangles each representing 50 games; 16 times 50 = 800.

QUESTION 37

The following graph indicates the number of computers sold each week at a store. Estimate the number of computers sold in a monthly period. A month is approximated to be four weeks.

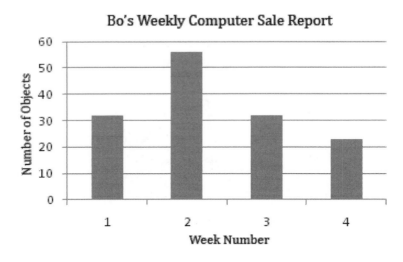

Bo's Weekly Computer Sale Report

A. 83
B. 97
C. 123
D. 143

Answer: D

Explanation: From the problem, it is known that a month is approximated to be four weeks. Add the value of the bars indicating the quantity of computers sold.

number of computer sold=week1+week2+week3+week4
number of computers sold=32+56+32+23=143 computers sold in a month

QUESTION 38

The following chart indicates the grade distribution in a college math class with 58 students. About how many students passed the class if at least a C grade is needed to accomplish this?

Percentage of Grades

A. 48 students
B. 45 students
C. 42 students
D. 40 students

Answer: B

Explanation: The total number of students is given as 58. In addition, the percentage of students that passed the class can be calculated by adding the percentages for A, B, and C grades.

$$\text{percentage of passing grades}=12.05\%+25.90\%+39.70\%=77.65\%$$

Convert this number to a decimal form. To do this, the percentage needs to be 100, or simply move the decimal point two units to the left to obtain the same result.

$$77.65\%=0.7765$$

Multiply the total number of students by the percentage written in decimal form.

$$\text{number of students who passed}=58\times0.7765=45.037$$
$$\text{number of students who passed}=45$$

QUESTION 39

Which of the following is the main cause of tide?

    A. wind
    B. gravity
    C. ocean currents
    D. rain

Answer: B

Explanation: Tides are the rise and fall of sea levels, and gravity is the main cause of tides.

QUESTION 40

In Northern hemisphere, surface currents always move water _____.

    A. clockwise
    B. counter-clockwise
    C. parallel
    D. horizontally

Answer: A

Explanation: Earth's rotation curls surface currents into giant clockwise whirlpools in the Northern Hemisphere.

QUESTION 41

The continental crust is the thickest beneath which of the following?

    A. mountains
    B. oceans
    C. plains
    D. forest

Answer: A

Explanation: The continental crust is the thickest beneath mountains.

QUESTION 42

_____ is the planet that could float on water due to its low density.

A. Venus
B. Mars
C. Saturn
D. Jupiter

Answer: C

Explanation: Saturn is the planet that could float on water due to its low density.

QUESTION 43

Of the following, which position of a roller coaster has the greatest amount of potential energy?

A. at the bottom of a hill
B. at the middle of a hill
C. as it travels up a hill
D. when at resting point

Answer: B

Explanation: Potential energy is greatest at the top of the hill, but no answer choice indicates that. The best answer choice is going to be the close to the top of the hill. At the middle of the hill is the greatest amount of potential energy of all the choices.

QUESTION 44

RNA is produced from DNA in the process of _____.

A. synthesis
B. replication
C. transcription
D. translation

Answer: C

Explanation: The first step of gene expression in transcription where particular segment of DNA is copied into RNA.

QUESTION 45

Which of the following would be the best use for a material that reflects almost all light?

- A. window
- B. mirror
- C. light paper
- D. black paper

Answer: B

Explanation: Mirror is a material that reflects almost all light.

QUESTION 46

Which of the following best describes mutation?

- A. a change that is inherited
- B. a change that is developed
- C. a change impacted later in life
- D. a controlling factor in plant growth

Answer: A

Explanation: Mutation is a natural process that changes a DNA sequence; this is an inherited change.

QUESTION 47

Which of the following is incorrectly described?

- A. circulatory system – breathing system
- B. digestive system – food processing system
- C. nervous system - transports messages
- D. muscular system – movement of the body

Answer: A

Explanation: The circulatory system is a network that carries blood throughout the body.

QUESTION 48

How does the human body maintain a constant temperature?

- A. homeostasis
- B. isotherm process
- C. release of energy
- D. intake of protein

Answer: A

Explanation: Homeostasis is what keeps human body at a constant temperature. Homeostasis is a property of a system in which a variable is active to remain at near equilibrium.

QUESTION 49

A fourth grade student sees a puddle of water on the sidewalk when she travels to school. As she travels back home, the puddle of water is gone. What happened to the water in the puddle?

- A. it disappears
- B. it freezes
- C. it condenses
- D. it evaporates

Answer: C

Explanation: Water is continually recycled in our environment through the process called the water cycle. The steps include evaporation, condensation, precipitation, and collection. Warmth causes evaporation to take place. The child in the problem sees a puddle on the way to school, but notices that it is gone on her way home from school. It is most probable that the temperature in the puddle increased throughout the day, causing the water to evaporate.

QUESTION 50

In the winter, the pond begins to freeze, causing the ducks to leave the pond to migrate to warmer climates. The ducks migrate because they have

    A. difficulty finding food

    B. too many enemies

    C. have to lay eggs near water

    D. too few places to hibernate

Answer: A

Explanation: Ducks get their food by hunting and scavenging in the water. So when the pond freezes, the ducks lose their food source, so they have to migrate to a warmer place where they can find food.

QUESTION 51

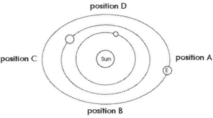

Where will the Earth (indicated by E) be in six months?

    A. near position D

    B. near position C

    C. near position B

    D. near position A

Answer: B

Explanation: Earth travels around the sun every 12 months. In six months, Earth will travel halfway around the sun. Position C is halfway around the sun from the Earth's starting position on the diagram. Near position C is correct.

QUESTION 52

Which is the first step in a design process?

    A. test the possible solutions
    B. revise the solution
    C. describe the problem
    D. identify possible solutions

Answer: C

Explanation: A problem has to be figured out (identified) and described before finding a solution to the problem. A problem that does not exist or has not been identified cannot have a solution.

QUESTION 53

The two students want classmates to repeat the investigation so that they can compare results.

When repeating an investigation, what should the students communicate so that the results may be compared?

    A. origin of the materials for model telephones
    B. materials and steps used in the investigation
    C. conclusions about results from first investigation
    D. communicate hypothesis

Answer: B

Explanation: To compare the results, the steps and material have to be the same. This will ensure that the comparison is valid.

QUESTION 54

In a lesson, the students will study how water changes from liquid to gas.

Materials: electric heating coil, beaker and thermometer

Procedure:

    A. Pour one liter of water into the beaker.
    B. Place the thermometer in the water.
    C. Record the temperature of the water.
    D. Place the beaker on the heating coil.
    E. Turn on the heating coil.
    F. Record the temperature of the water every minute for 10 minutes.

Of the following, what can be done to ensure safety in this experiment?

    I.   slowly pour water into beaker
    II.   keep close distance from hot heating coil
    III.   ensure outside of the glass beaker is not wet

    A. I only
    B. I and II
    C. I and III
    D. I, II, and III

Answer: C

Explanation: Pouring water slowly and ensuring outside of the glass beaker is not wet are safety procedures to undertake.

QUESTION 55

Which weather observation is likely just before a heavy snowstorm?

A. clear sky
B. thick gray clouds
C. small white clouds
D. warm temperature

Answer: B

Explanation: Cumulonimbus clouds, which are dark and gray, are in the sky before it starts to snow.

QUESTION 56

Butterflies obtain food from the flowers of a plant. They also lay their eggs on the leaves of the plant. As the caterpillars develop, they eat the leaves. Plants benefit from the butterflies as the butterflies

A. help add nutrients to the nectar of the flowers
B. help pollinate flowers so that seeds can form
C. help the plant grow larger flowers
D. help grow the plants leaves

Answer: B

Explanation: Butterflies are active during the day, and butterflies help pollinate flowers so that seeds can form.

QUESTION 57

A student took two ice cubes from the freezer and put them in a glass of freshly squeezed kiwi fruit juice. After 15 minutes, the student tried to take the ice cubes out of the juice, but there were gone. What type of change took place?

    A. chemical, because the ice cubes became a new substance
    B. physical, because the ice cubes evaporated
    C. chemical, because the ice cubes' energy became heat
    D. physical, because the ice cubes changed into liquid

Answer: D

Explanation: The chemical is the same, so there is no chemical change; option A and C are eliminated. No evaporation occurred, so option B is eliminated. Option D is correct. Physical change occurred as the ice cubes changed into liquid.

QUESTION 58

Soil in an empty field blows away during a strong wind. Which activity slows the erosion of this field over time?

    A. building fence
    B. watering
    C. plowing
    D. planting grass

Answer: D

Explanation: Erosion is the act in which earth is worn away, often by water, wind, or ice. Planting grass will slow the erosion of the empty field.

QUESTION 59

What makes a plant bend toward the light?

- A. phototropism
- B. photosynthesis
- C. cellular respiration
- D. convection

Answer: A

Explanation: Phototropism is the orientation of a plant in response to light. Photoropism can make a plant bend toward the light.

QUESTION 60

Engaging the entire family in a healthy eating plan is most likely the best approach in which of the following?

- A. Supporting elementary students to eating healthy.
- B. Supporting an adolescent in losing weight.
- C. Teaching kids on importance of eating healthy.
- D. Supporting state curriculum of teaching healthy eating at home.

Answer: B

Explanation: Engaging the whole family is the best approach in supporting the adolescent to lose weight because the student lives with their family most of the time and the family can encourage them to lose weight.

QUESTION 61

In which of the following can sound waves not travel in?

   A. a vacuum.
   B. air
   C. water
   D. building

Answer: A

Explanation: Sound is unable to travel through a vacuum or in outer space. The reason for this is because time is a vibration of matter.

QUESTION 62

An object moves in the direction in which the force is applied. The previous statement is an example of

   A. potential energy
   B. power
   C. work
   D. inertia

Answer: C

Explanation: Work is force times distance, which is related to the first sentence of the question.

QUESTION 63

Which scientific law states that a body accelerates in the direction of the net force applied?

   A. Newton's first law
   B. Newton's second law
   C. Boyle's law
   D. Faraday's law

Answer: B

Explanation: Newton's second law states that a body accelerates in the direction of the net force applied.

QUESTION 64

    I.   to respond readily to instructions

    II.   to follow rules, codes, and safety practices

    III.   to work with other students to ensure learning

    IV.   to warm up and recover from exercise

Which of the following are ways to teach students on ensuring safe practices are being implemented in physical education classrooms?

A. I and II
B. II and III
C. I, II, and IV
D. II, III, and IV

Answer: C

Explanation: Working with other students to ensure learning is not related to ensuring safe practices occurs in physical education classrooms. All other options have a connection to ensuring safety in physical education classrooms.

QUESTION 65

What is the difference between weight and mass?

A. mass is the amount of matter in an object while weight is measurement of the gravitational pull on an object
B. mass is the amount of particles in an object while weight is measurement of the gravitational pull away an object
C. mass is the measure of the total object while measurement is the measure of the object with gravitational pull
D. mass is the amount of matter in while weight is measurement of the dimension of the object

Answer: A

Explanation: Mass is the amount of matter in an object while weight is measurement of the gravitational pull on an object.

QUESTION 66

In design, which of the following is common challenge of complex systems?

    A. closed loop system

    B. many parts and connections

    C. open loop system

    D. increase cost of designing

Answer: B

Explanation: The keyword in the question is "complex." The system is going to be consisting of many parts and connections, which is a common challenge.

QUESTION 67

For an unordered system to become more ordered, which of the following is required?

    A. increase in pressure

    B. expenditure of energy

    C. increase in the size of the system

    D. increase in heat

Answer: B

Explanation: An unordered system has too much energy. Some of the energy needs to be released, which is indicated by option B.

QUESTION 68

A pitcher plant traps insects in a pitcher-shaped leaf from which the insect is unable to escape. Which of the following best describes the reason for this strategy?

    A. allow the plant more carbohydrates

    B. attract more insects

    C. help the plant survive

    D. dissuade insect predation

Answer: B

Explanation: The intention of a trap of a pitcher-shaped leaf is to attract more insects. This will trap more insects trapped to support the life of leafs.

QUESTION 69

A basketball rolls down an incline and then goes on to a flat, smooth surface until it stops. Which of the following best explains why the ball came to a halt?

    A. The weight of the ball caused it to stop.

    B. The frictional forces overcame the ball's inertia.

    C. There was no gravity force on the flat surface.

    D. The potential energy was gone when ball was on the flat surface.

Answer: B

Explanation: Frictional forces exist as the ball is rolling. Friction is a force that is created when two surfaces move or try to move across each other. Friction always opposes the motion or attempted motion of one surface across another surface. The frictional forces overcame the ball's inertia, which stops the ball.

QUESTION 70

Which of the following is the main cause of the sun having high temperatures?

    A. nuclear fusion reactions

    B. nuclear fission reactions

    C. chemical reactions

    D. angular momentum

Answer: A

Explanation: Fusion reactions power the Sun and other stars. Nuclear fusion reactions are the main cause of the sun having high temperatures.

QUESTION 71

While working on a class physics experiment, Juan dropped a glass test tube filled with an unknown liquid. What should Juan do first?

    A. clean up the spill

    B. inform the teacher

    C. walk away

    D. put on gloves

Answer: B

Explanation: The first step is to inform the teacher, so the teacher can take the necessary steps for proper handling. Juan should not walk away as someone else can come near the unknown liquid.

QUESTION 72

Which of the following biogeochemical cycles is most impacted by the erosion of limestone?

  A. the water cycle
  B. the carbon cycle
  C. the oxygen cycle
  D. none of the above

Answer: B

Explanation: The carbon cycle, which exists in the ground, sea, plants, animals, and the air, is the movement of carbon through the environment. Erosion of limestone impacts the carbon cycle the most.

QUESTION 73

  I.   rust forming on an outcrop of iron-rich rock
  II.   limestone dissolving
  III. melting water

Of the above, which of the following is/are shows of chemical weathering involving oxygen?

  A. I only
  B. I and II
  C. I and III
  D. I, II, and III

Answer: A

Explanation: The only option that shows chemical weathering involving oxygen is rust forming on an outcrop of iron-rich rock. Chemical weathering is the erosion or disintegration of rocks, building materials, etc., caused by chemical reactions.

QUESTION 74

What type of dance involves individuals holding hands in a circle?

    A. chain dance
    B. folk dance
    C. ballroom dance
    D. modern dance

Answer: A

Explanation: Circle dance, also known as chain dance, is a style of dance done in a circle or semicircle with holding hands.

QUESTION 75

What is the term for light and dark areas on paintings?

    A. chiaroscuro
    B. value
    C. color
    D. illusion

Answer: A

Explanation: Chiaroscuro is the treatment of light and shade in drawing and painting.

OAE 019 Elementary Education Subtest II

Mathematics, Science, Arts, Health, and Fitness

By: Preparing Teachers In America™

10053647R00101

Made in the USA
Lexington, KY
19 September 2018